JOE PAPROCKI

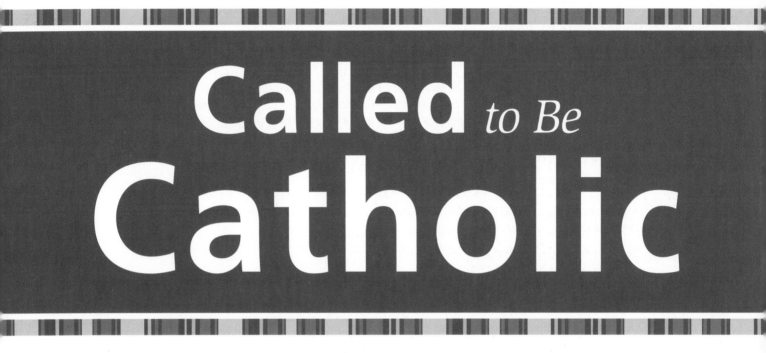

Called *to Be* Catholic

ESSENTIALS OF THE CATHOLIC FAITH FOR AGES 12–15

LOYOLAPRESS.
A JESUIT MINISTRY
Chicago

IMPRIMATUR

In accordance with c. 827, permission to publish is granted on April 20, 2012 by Rev. Msgr. John F. Canary, Vicar General of the Archdiocese of Chicago. Permission to publish is an official declaration of ecclesiastical authority that the material is free from doctrinal and moral error. No legal responsibility is assumed by the grant of this permission.

Grateful acknowledgment is given to authors, publishers, photographers, museums, and agents for permission to reprint the copyrighted material contained herein. Every effort has been made to determine copyright owners. In the case of any omissions, the publisher will be pleased to make suitable acknowledgments in future editions. Acknowledgments begin on page 105.

Advisers: Jeannette L. Graham, M.A.; Jim Manney
Cover design: Loyola Press
Cover Illustration: iStockPhoto.com/Keith Bishop (Crucifix), Veer/PicsFive (background)
Interior design: Loyola Press

ISBN-13: 978-0-8294-3677-8
ISBN-10: 0-8294-3677-4

Printed in the United States of America.

LOYOLA PRESS.
A JESUIT MINISTRY

3441 N. Ashland Avenue
Chicago, Illinois 60657
(800) 621-1008
www.loyolapress.com

20 21 22 23 24 Web 10 9 8 7 6 5 4 3

contents

pray

Come, Holy Spirit, fill the hearts of your faithful.

And kindle in them the fire of your love.

Send forth your Spirit and they shall be created.

And you shall renew the face of the earth.

Let us pray:

O God, by the light of the Holy Spirit you have taught the hearts of your faithful. In the same Spirit, help us to know what is truly right and always to rejoice in your consolation.

We ask this through Christ, Our Lord. Amen.

MY PRAYER

A journey of a thousand miles begins with a single step.

Write a prayer to God, reflecting on where you are in your faith journey at this moment. Think about the questions, hopes, fears, and desires you have, then begin a conversation with God. That will be your starting point—your single step for this journey.

I, _____, am about to begin a

journey to explore the foundations of my Catholic faith and to

deepen my relationship with God. This is my prayer:

_____

_____

_____

_____

_____

_____

_____

CALLED TO BE CATHOLIC
Welcome Letter

DEAR YOUNG PERSON,

I bet if you put your mind to it, you could quickly and easily make a list of five or ten things you know about your best friend: his or her favorite song, food, movie, hobby, team, and so on. You can probably describe some things about his or her past, some of your friend's accomplishments, and interests, what angers him or her, what your friend believes most deeply, and what his or her hopes and dreams are. When someone is important to us, we make a point of getting to know more about him or her. The more we know about someone, the more we truly know this person as a friend.

Jesus once said, "I no longer call you servants, I call you friends." What a gift to have a friend like Jesus! One of the ways that you can deepen your friendship with Jesus is by learning more about him: what he is most interested in, what his hopes are, what angers him, and what he believes in most deeply. You can also get to know Jesus by learning about the things he said and did. This book, *Called to Be Catholic,* is going to help you do just that. By learning about Jesus, you will be able to relate to him as a friend and enable that friendship to grow and deepen.

There's a great Christian hymn called "What a Friend We Have in Jesus." I hope you recognize what a friend you have in Jesus and that you take the time to get to know more about him and come to know him personally. Your life will never be the same!

Sincerely,

Joe Paprocki

Joe Paprocki, D.Min.
National Consultant for Faith Formation, Loyola Press

Foundations of Our
faith

What are some qualities that make someone a good friend? Is it someone who is a good listener, kind, and loyal? What makes you a good friend to others? Now think about your relationship with God. How would you describe that relationship?

Then Jesus approached and said to them, "All power in heaven and on earth has been given to me. Go, therefore, and make disciples of all nations, baptizing them in the name of the Father, and of the Son, and of the holy Spirit . . ."
—Matthew 28:18–19

God in Your Life

Your days are probably filled with people demanding your attention: friends, parents, siblings, teachers, coaches, teammates, and neighbors. All these people offer ideas about what it takes to live a good life. They say: Get an education. Treat others well. Learn how to work hard. Develop your talents. Play fair. Find good friends. Be a good friend.

These things are important, but the Catholic Church says that the one thing that is more important than anything else is a connection with God. The basic message of the Gospel is that God loves you and wants to have a relationship with you. *Gospel* means "good news." The idea that God wants to be part of your life is very good news.

What Makes a Relationship Good?

God wants to have a close relationship with you. How does this work? Think about how you relate to your best friends. Most likely, four elements are present.

- You **know** certain things about your friends. They like you, and you can trust them.

- You **do** things together. You have fun when you spend time together.

- You **act** like a friend. You behave respectfully, show affection, and share your possessions with one another.

- You **communicate.** You talk with them and share your hopes and dreams with one another. You also share the difficult things.

Four Pillars of a Relationship with God

Four elements are also present in our relationship with God. Think about them as pillars, or columns, holding up a roof of a large building.

- **Creed:** What we *know* about our faith in God

- **Sacraments:** How we *celebrate* our faith in God

- **The Moral Life:** How we *live out* our faith in God

- **Prayer:** How we *communicate* with God

When you get these pillars in place, you'll have a strong foundation with God—the most important relationship you will ever have.

MY TURN: My Prayer

There are many ways to pray. List some of the ways you pray.

_____

_____

_____

_____

_____

We already know a lot about God. God has told us much about what he is like, what he has done for us, and what he wants. We find this in the **Creed** of the Catholic Church, the Bible, and in the ancient traditions of the Catholic faith. We hold on to our faith that is revealed to us through Scripture and Tradition and is summarized in the Creed.

We express our love for God through participation in the liturgy and sacraments of the Church. The **sacraments** are the most important ways that God shows his love for us.

We act lovingly toward God and other people. The **Ten Commandments,** the **Beatitudes,** and Jesus' moral teachings show us how to live lives of peace, justice, and love. We live our faith according to Catholic morality.

We communicate with God in prayer. The Church teaches us how to pray together at Mass and other times of worship, and also how to pray by ourselves.

God Reaches Out

Most of the time, you have to work hard to get what you want. Do you want to be good at a sport? Then you do what the coach says, watch what you eat, play hard, and—above all—practice, practice, practice. Do you want to make new friends? This usually takes some time and work as you reach out to others and prove yourself as someone worthy of being a friend. Do you want to excel in school? Hit the books. Study. Whatever it may be, decide what you want, and then go after it.

With God it's the other way around. God takes the first step, and he continues to reach out to us as our connection with him deepens and grows stronger. We hold up our end of the relationship when we work in response to God's invitation to know him and love him. God issues an invitation; we answer the call.

Since the beginning of time, God has been inviting human beings into a relationship with him; from the beginning of time, people have answered this invitation in some way.

together

It's Not About You

As we grow in a relationship with God, a surprising thing happens. We pay less attention to ourselves and dedicate more time and energy to God and to the people God has put in our lives. Don't misunderstand—you are a very important person. God cares deeply about you; he's personally concerned about your life. But part of our answer to God's invitation is to turn more of our attention to what God wants and what God is doing.

For thousands of years, human beings thought that the earth was the center of everything. Every day we could watch the sun rise in the east and set in the west. It seemed obvious that the sun revolved around the earth. But about 500 years ago, it was shown beyond a doubt that the earth was circling the sun. We've since learned that the earth and the sun are tiny specks in a vast universe of billions of stars. Knowing this makes us humble.

The same kind of shift in thinking happens as we get to know God. It's easy to think that we're the center of our world. It's a pleasant thought, and it's reinforced constantly in our society in many ways, even by parents and teachers. But the center of our world is God and what he is doing in our lives.

The person who knew this best was Jesus, the Son of God. During his life on earth, his driving passion was to do his Father's will. "[N]ot my will but yours be done," he told his Father. (Luke 22:42) We say the same thing every time we pray the Lord's Prayer, the prayer Jesus taught us, praying "thy will be done on earth as it is in heaven."

MY TURN: Friendship

Think of all the people you consider good friends. What qualities do these people share?

_____

_____

_____

_____

_____

God's Revelation

God has told us much about who he is and how we can know and love him. **Revelation** is what we know about God. Much of it is written down. Much of it consists of traditions of beliefs and teachings that stretch back thousands of years. The Catholic Church preserves this Revelation and teaches what it means.

The most important Revelation of God is Jesus Christ, who is both fully God and fully man. Jesus lived the model human life. He showed us how to pray, how to love one another, and how to serve. Through his suffering, Death, and Resurrection, Jesus delivered the human race from its burden of sin. Jesus' work of saving and healing the world continues through the Church and through the work of every person who strives to love and serve God.

The Catholic **faith** is about who Jesus was, what he taught, and what he did. Having faith means believing in Jesus' teaching and trusting him to guide your life.

Scripture and Tradition

God's Revelation comes in two forms: **Scripture**, the written word of God, and **Tradition,** the teaching of Jesus' disciples. Jesus is the source of both Scripture and Tradition.

Scripture is the Bible, the written Word of God. More copies of the Bible have been printed than any other book in history. It tells the story of God's relationship with people from the creation of the world to the first Christian communities and to the establishment of the Church in the first century. The Old Testament tells the story of the Jewish people. The New Testament is the story of Jesus and the early Church.

You hear readings from both the Old and New Testaments at Mass. These readings are some of the most important parts of the Bible, but there is much more in the Bible to read and consider.

The teaching of Jesus and his Apostles is also passed along through the Tradition of the Church. Tradition doesn't mean doing the same things over and over while everything else changes. The Church's Tradition is the teaching of Jesus, passed on by his Apostles, preserved through the centuries by the Church, and lived out in our time.

SACRED SIGN: The Bible

The Bible, the sacred book of the Christian faith, is composed of 73 books of different types. The central part of the Old Testament is the *Pentateuch,* five historical books that tell the story of Creation and the origins of the Jewish people. The central part of the New Testament is the Gospels of Matthew, Mark, Luke, and John. They tell the story of Jesus.

THE HOLY BIBLE

Revelation from Scripture: Ten Commandments and Eight Beatitudes

God's Revelation in both the Old and New Testaments is the basis for Catholic teaching on living a moral life.

One of the most important of these moral teachings is found in the Old Testament. There we learn that God gave the Ten Commandments to the Jewish people through their great leader Moses, who delivered them from slavery in Egypt. The First Commandment is to love and serve God above all things. The remaining commandments forbid murder, stealing, lying, and other forms of wrong behavior.

In the New Testament, one of the best summaries of Jesus' teaching about right and wrong is the Beatitudes, part of the Sermon on the Mount. While the Ten Commandments mainly forbid sinful behavior, Jesus paid particular attention to the virtues and attitudes of a person's heart. The first beatitude is "Blessed are the poor in spirit, for theirs is the kingdom of heaven." (Matthew 5:3) Other beatitudes praise those who seek justice, who make peace, and who give mercy.

Revelation from Tradition: The Creed

An important Revelation from Tradition is the Nicene Creed, a summary of what Christians believe about God the Father, Son, and Holy Spirit. The Creed is prayed aloud at Masses that are celebrated on Sundays and major feast days. The Nicene Creed begins, "I believe in one God, the Father almighty, maker of heaven and earth, of all things visible and invisible." This Creed is an ancient text, written in the fourth century A.D. by the bishops of the Church in the cities of Nicaea and Constantinople. Over the centuries, the Church has affirmed the Creed as *orthodox*, meaning "correct belief."

RITE: Baptism

During the Rite of Baptism, the bishop, priest, or deacon pours water three times over the head of the candidate or immerses the candidate in the water three times. As the candidate is immersed or the water is poured over his or her head, the celebrant says, "I baptize you in the name of the Father, and of the Son, and of the Holy Spirit." The water in Baptism symbolizes our sins being washed away.

Authority You Can Trust

How do we know that Scripture and Tradition are true? It comes down to trusting the authority of God. You respect the authority of teachers and parents because you've learned to trust them. The direction they give you has good results, and most times, what they tell you turns out to be true. When it comes to faith, all authority comes from God. God the Father gave all authority to his Son, Jesus Christ. Jesus said, "All power in heaven and on earth has been given to me." (Matthew 28:18) Jesus established the Church and gave the Apostles and their successors, the bishops, authority to preach and teach in his name: "Go, therefore, and make disciples of all nations . . ." (Matthew 28:19)

God doesn't deceive or lie. He is love and truth. God came into our world in the person of Jesus Christ, who proclaimed the Gospel—the truth about God and the truth about how to live in peace and love. The Church preserves what Jesus said and helps us follow Jesus' teaching and example.

God has reached out to you—showing you the way to know him and love him. The Way is Jesus. Jesus Christ is alive in our world today, especially in the Church he established. God himself says this. And God's is a word you can trust.

WITNESS: Abraham

About two-thousand of years before Jesus was born, God called Abraham from his home and invited him to journey through the desert to the land of Canaan. Abraham, along with his wife Sarah, accepted this call and showed great faith in God through many trials. Abraham is the founding patriarch of the Jewish people and a spiritual father to Christians.

MY TURN: Authority

Think of the people in your life whom you look up to and are in a position of authority. What makes them trustworthy?

_____

_____

_____

_____

summary

FAITH SUMMARY

God wants us to be in a relationship with him. Jesus Christ is the most important way in which God reveals himself to us. We can look to Scripture and the Church to guide us in ways to grow closer to God. We depend on the Creed, the sacraments, the moral life, and prayer to help us grow closer to God through the Church.

REMEMBER

What are the four pillars of a relationship with God?
The Creed, the sacraments, the moral life, and prayer are the four pillars of a relationship with God.

What are the two forms of God's Revelation?
Scripture and the Church's living Tradition are the two forms of God's Revelation.

What does having faith mean?
Having faith means believing in Jesus' teaching and trusting him to guide your life.

Who established the Church?
The Catholic Church was established by Jesus and teaches with his authority.

REACH OUT

1. Think of lonely people you're aware of—at school, in your neighborhood, maybe even in your family. Resolve to do something to reach out to one of them. Write what you could do.

2. Where do you most need help in your life right now? When you get some time alone, pray a prayer asking Jesus for guidance during this time in your life.

Words to Know

Beatitudes	sacraments
Creed	Scripture
faith	Ten Commandments
Revelation	Tradition

REFLECT

Think about the faith Jesus has in us, his followers. How have you shown your faith in others? Write about a time you demonstrated faith in others.

_____

_____

_____

_____

_____

_____

_____

_____

_____

_____

_____

Jesus, I want to know you better. Come into my heart. Help me. Help the people I love. Teach me what I need to know. Amen.

United in love

Recall a time when you felt something "click," like a math problem or a sports skill. How did you feel at first? Scared? Confused? How did you feel after it "clicked" for you? Confident? Excited? Seeing a challenge with new eyes helps us realize that what seems difficult at first just takes time and understanding.

After all the people had been baptized and Jesus also had been baptized and was praying, heaven was opened and the holy Spirit descended upon him in bodily form like a dove. And a voice came from heaven, "You are my beloved Son; with you I am well pleased."   *–Luke 3:21–22*

Three Persons in One God

The Trinity is important because it tells us some surprising things about who God is and what God is like. Your relationship with God is the most important relationship in your life. You learned about the four pillars of faith in the last chapter: We *learn* about God (Creed), we *receive* God's love (sacraments), we *live* the way God wants us to (the moral life), and we *connect* with God (prayer). It's all about getting to know God, and the fact that God is Father, Son, and Spirit is the first and deepest thing to know about him.

Getting to Know God

Wherever Catholics get together, you'll find mention of the **Trinity.** You don't even have to be paying much attention to notice it. Every Mass begins with "In the name of the Father, and of the Son, and of the Holy Spirit." Catholics frequently say these words as they make the **Sign of the Cross.** Many hymns and prayers end by honoring the Father, Son, and Holy Spirit. Sometimes when you're watching a soccer or baseball game on television, you'll see a player make the Sign of the Cross after scoring a goal or hitting a home run.

Think about the Trinity for a moment. We believe that there is one God, but that he is Three Persons: Father, Son, and Holy Spirit. The Trinity is *the* central mystery of the Christian faith. Billions of people on earth believe in God, but only Christians believe in a God who is Father, Son, and Holy Spirit. It makes us unique.

The Doctrine of the Trinity

Theologians have written millions of words about the doctrine of the Trinity. Their books would fill entire libraries. But the Christian teaching about the Trinity boils down to three main points.

- **God is One.** Christians do not believe in three gods. Like Jews and Muslims, we believe that there is one God—the Creator of Heaven and earth.

MY TURN: Explaining the Trinity

Saint Patrick used a shamrock plant to explain the Trinity. Think of a way you could explain the Trinity.

_____

_____

_____

_____

_____

rela

- **God is Father, Son, and Spirit.** The one God exists in Three Persons. Each Person is distinct; each is wholly God. Human beings didn't come up with the Trinity on their own—God revealed himself as Three Persons through Jesus, his Son, and through the Holy Spirit.

- **The differences have to do with relationships.** God is a community of Persons. The Father is Father because he has a Son. The Son is Son because he has a Father. Their love together is expressed as the Holy Spirit, who brings God's life and truth into the world.

thinking about them. You watch what they do and listen to what they say. You know they're loyal when they stick with you in tough times. You know they're generous when they surprise you with a gift. You know they like you when they spend time with you. You know they are wise when they give you good advice. At the same time, you never know *everything* about your friends.

So it is with God. We know him by his words and actions. God told the Hebrew people that there is only one God, not many, as human beings had previously thought. With Jesus came another surprise. God had a Son, which meant he was Father as well. Jesus said, "The Father and I are one." (John 10:30) Then came the Third Person, the Holy Spirit. Jesus said, "Receive the holy Spirit." (John 20:22) Here is the mystery of the Trinity—three distinct Persons, yet one God.

How Do We Know About the Trinity?

We wouldn't know about the Trinity unless God told us about it. It comes from God's Revelation—the holy Scriptures and the living Tradition of the Church, which we talked about in the first chapter. Our natural human ability to think and figure things out can tell us many things about God. For example, almost all people believe that there *is* a God. Every human society we know about has a way of worshiping God. But the knowledge that God exists in Three Persons isn't something we know by using our heads. God tells us about it.

God reveals the Trinity to us through his words and actions. It's like getting to know your friends. You don't know your friends by

We know God as Father, Son, and Holy Spirit through Scripture and Tradition. The Hebrew people watched how the one God took care of them, and they listened to what God said about himself. In Jesus, people met God in human flesh. They observed his miracles and listened to his teaching. They watched how he treated people. They wept when he was killed, and they were astounded when he rose from the dead. We know about Jesus through the New Testament and the living Tradition of the Church.

What Does the Trinity Tell Us About God?

God Is Father

The fact that God is **Father** means that he is the Creator. All things begin with him. God's Fatherhood also means that he protects and cares for his creation, especially human beings.

Father is a good word for God, but it's not the perfect word. For one thing, it brings to mind earthly fathers. For another, it may suggest that God is male. You've probably seen artists' paintings of God shown as a powerful, older man with a beard and flowing white hair. God is Father, but he isn't a man. We call God *Father* because this is the name Jesus revealed to us. The Bible also tells us that God has qualities that are traditionally associated with motherhood. God, however, is neither male or female. God is God, beyond gender, race, or any other human category. When we pray as a Church, however, we use the title *Father* because that is the title revealed to us by Jesus.

God Is Son

The Father has a **Son**—Jesus, who lived about two thousand years ago in an out-of-the-way province of the Roman Empire. Jesus is the most important way we know about God. Jesus shows God to be merciful, loving, generous, and just. He loves us so much that he died for us. You and Jesus have the same Father. That means Jesus is your brother.

God Is Holy Spirit

The **Holy Spirit** is the active presence of God in our lives. The Spirit "proceeds" from the Father and Son—that is, the Spirit is an expression of their love. Through the Spirit, God is living and active in the world.

MY TURN: What Do You Need from God?

What are some issues or things on your mind lately?

_____

_____

How might God the Father, Son, and Holy Spirit take care of these needs?

_____

_____

_____

A God We Can Know

Changes in life often seem huge and sometimes downright scary. Recall some of the changes you may have experienced: starting a new school; moving to a new neighborhood or city; the first days playing on a new team; learning a new skill like drawing or a musical instrument or algebra. Chances are the new situation seemed difficult and mysterious. You thought you might not be able to do it.

Chances are, though, that most things worked out pretty well, or at least better than you expected. You made friends, mastered the new skill, felt at home in the new place and as a result, your world expanded.

So it is with getting to know God. God at first may seem confusing and difficult to wrap your head around. It's hard to see how we can get along well with a God like this. That's why many people wonder how they can relate to a God they don't feel they fully understand.

It turns out that God is very different. God is always available to you and for you, and you can come to God whenever you feel like it. God is a community of love, just as your family, friends, and parish are a community. God comes to us in relationships, just as you have relationships from the time you get up in the morning to the time you go to bed at night. God is love. This is what we mean by the doctrine of the Trinity.

So what is God like? Think about the people in your life and what you need from them. Every day you need protection, care, and support. This is what your parents and family give you. This is what God gives you too, because God is the perfect Father. Every day you need friendship, affection, and guidance. This is what you have in Jesus, your brother, the Son of God. Every day you need the strength to do good work. This is what you have through God the Holy Spirit, the active power of God in your daily life.

SACRED SIGN: Dove

The Holy Spirit is often depicted as a dove. This tradition is based on the account of Jesus' baptism, where we read "the holy Spirit descended upon him in bodily form like a dove." (Luke 3:22) The dove is also a symbol of peace. This too is based on Scripture. In the ark, Noah learned that land was near when he saw a dove carrying an olive branch. (Genesis 8:11)

What the Trinity Tells Us About Ourselves

Imagine that you are at a family get-together, and your aunt says that you've got your father's eyes or your mother's hair. Has a friend ever told you that you act just like your brother or sister? Maybe you don't like comments like these because you want to be yourself, not your father or mother or brother or sister. But it's true that family members resemble one another. It's also true that we look like God.

The opening chapters of the Book of Genesis, the first book of the Bible, say that God created human beings in his "image and likeness." This is another mystery that we can't fully understand, but the basic idea is clear enough. We resemble God and God resembles us. Since God is Trinity—Father, Son, and Spirit—what does this tell us about ourselves?

Unity

Let's go back to that family get-together. Everyone's different, but everyone has something in common too. You're part of a family. You're united with other people in this family even though every person in your family is very much himself or herself. Unity—it's a joyful feeling. You feel it in a cheering crowd, when you're having a great time with your best friends, when you're playing on a team that's winning, when you're making music with other people in a choir or a band.

The Trinity explains why we feel this way. We resemble God. God is one, yet he is three distinct Persons. We are distinct people, yet we love unity. The desire for it is placed deep

---

RITE: The Sign of the Cross

Catholics frequently touch their head, chest, and shoulders while praying the words, "In the name of the Father, and of the Son, and of the Holy Spirit." When we make this gesture, we honor the Three Persons of the Trinity while remembering Jesus' sacrifice on the cross. This "Sign of the Cross" is an ancient prayer that calls on God to bless and protect us.

in our hearts. Our hunger for unity will be fully satisfied when we're united with God in Heaven. In the meantime, we can find unity within our parish, which serves as a community of believers. When we come together to praise and worship God, we are experiencing something of God.

Love

Love and unity go hand in hand. Saint Augustine, one of the greatest leaders of the early Church, said that people are united when they agree about the love they share. You feel one with your family because you love the people in it. You can lose yourself in good times with your friends because you love them. Even when your interests differ from someone, say in taste in music or how you dress or what you read, you still love him or her. Having different likes and dislikes adds to our personalities, but deep down, we're all made in the same way. We have love for others and love for ourselves, just as God intended.

We love because God loves. The doctrine of the Trinity means that love is at the very heart of God. God is a community of love—Father, Son, and Spirit. Because we are like God, we can love too.

WITNESS: Saint Patrick

In the fifth century A.D., Saint Patrick led the missionary work that converted most of the Irish people to Christianity. He is the patron saint of Ireland. March 17, his feast day, is a popular celebration, particularly in places where the Irish have settled. Saint Patrick is said to have used a shamrock, a three-leaf clover, to illustrate how three divine Persons are one in the Trinity.

MY TURN: United in Love

Recall a time when you felt especially united with other people. Briefly describe this experience.

_____

_____

_____

_____

_____

summary

FAITH SUMMARY

The Trinity is one way of understanding God and his role in our lives. The Trinity is Three Persons in one: God the Father, Jesus the Son, and the Holy Spirit. God is revealed to us through Scripture and Tradition. The Trinity helps us recognize that God is one but Three distinct Persons, much like how we are many things but are also members of the Church.

REMEMBER

What are the three most important points in the doctrine of the Trinity?

There is one God. God is Three Persons— Father, Son, and Spirit. The differences among these Persons are a matter of relationships.

How do we know about the Trinity?

We know God as Father, Son, and Spirit through God's words and actions. These are found in Scripture and the living Tradition of the Church.

What does it mean to call God Father?

God the Father is the Creator and protector. He gave us life, and he cares for his creation.

What does it mean to call God Son?

The Son of God is Jesus Christ. Jesus' words and deeds are the most important way we learn about God.

Who is God the Holy Spirit?

The Holy Spirit is the active presence of God in our world today.

REACH OUT

1. Think about the people you know who need God's help. Ask God to bless them.

2. Think about who in your life has had a positive impact on you. Write what qualities these people have that make them special to you.

Words to Know

Father	Son
Holy Spirit	theologians
Sign of the Cross	Trinity

REFLECT

Spend some time thinking about the good people and things in your life. Write about why you like these people and places and things.

_____

_____

_____

_____

_____

_____

Lord God, thank you for my family and my friends. They care for me and love me and are forgiving when I do not act kindly toward them. Help me realize when I am wrong and thank them for being in my life. Bless them all, in the name of the Father, and of the Son, and of the Holy Spirit. Amen.

Source of Our
redemption

Recall a time when you felt helpless to change a bad situation. Perhaps a friend was being treated unfairly, or maybe you were blamed for something you didn't do. What did you do in that situation? Do you wish you could have reacted differently? How would you handle tough situations in the future?

But now Christ has been raised from the dead, the firstfruits of those who have fallen asleep. For since death came through a human being, the resurrection of the dead came also through a human being. For just as in Adam all die, so too in Christ shall all be brought to life. *–1 Corinthians 15:20–22*

Something Is Wrong

You've probably seen photos of planet Earth taken from space. The world is beautiful—a lovely globe with deep blue oceans and shimmering white clouds set against the darkness of space. No wonder at the beginning, God looked at the world he created and said that it is good.

But something's wrong with the world now. It's full of pain and suffering. It's marred by natural disasters like tsunamis and hurricanes as well as man-made disasters like war and poverty. In our own lives, things often go badly as well. We do hurtful or senseless things. Sometimes people let us down, and other times, we let people down.

Why is the world this way? It's puzzling. You're going to be wrestling with the unhappiness in the world all through your life. It is very important to understand why things are the way they are and what God has done to repair the situation. The word *Gospel* means "good news." This chapter is about why the news is so good.

What's the Problem?

Take a look around your world. Notice the bully who threatens others or the kid who mocks and laughs at their troubles. Notice the people who tell lies about others or the teen who scorns school, church, classmates, teachers, and parents. Notice the sneak, the thief, the cheater.

Look at the world around you. People are poor, ill, neglected, lonely. Some people are disrespected because of their skin color, their language, their dress, their culture.

Sometimes good people suffer while corrupt people prosper. Violence is too common in our neighborhoods and communities.

The traditional word for all this is **sin.** Sin is a separation from doing what God intends for us. Most sin is people doing things like stealing a few dollars and telling little lies. We're not satisfied with what we have; we want what other people have. But a lot of what we call sin is something more profound, deeper—more like a sickness. There are times when we want

MY TURN: Making Things Right

Why do you think it can sometimes be difficult to overcome temptation?

_____

_____

_____

_____

_____

_____

to do good, and yet something prevents us from doing it. Sometimes we do whatever we like and don't think about the consequences or who is affected by our actions. Saint Augustine, a great leader of the early Church, tells a story about one day when he and some friends stole pears from an orchard. They didn't want the pears; they fed them to some pigs. What they wanted was to do something *bad.*

Original Sin

At the very beginning of the human race, God created man and woman to live in harmony with him and each other. Adam and Eve, our first parents, turned away from God and followed their own will instead of God's. The human race has suffered the consequences of this bad decision ever since. This is called **Original Sin.**

God told Adam and Eve not to eat fruit from the tree in the center of the garden. They ate the fruit anyway, tempted by the devil's promise that it would make them "like gods." As punishment, God drove Adam and Eve from paradise. (Genesis 3:1–24)

What the Story Means

This story uses figurative language to make its point. The sin of Adam and Eve wasn't eating a piece of fruit. It was their decision to live a life separate from God. God didn't punish them; they punished themselves by the choice they made. It's no surprise that they discovered that a life without God was not a happy life.

The Adam and Eve story is about losing paradise. Once we were secure with God, now we've lost touch with him. The sense of having lost paradise is planted deep in our hearts.

That's a consequence of Original Sin. Once we were home; now we are lost.

It's important not to confuse Original Sin with other kinds of sins. We are personally responsible for our own sins—lying, stealing, cheating, fighting, and other wrong actions. But we're not personally responsible for Original Sin. Original Sin is a condition into which we're born. It's about something that's *missing,* about being separated from God.

The Consequences of Original Sin

Original Sin did not just affect Adam and Eve. Hundreds of years later, we are still experiencing the consequences today.

First, our idea of God became warped. Adam and Eve did wrong, but it didn't occur to them to ask for forgiveness. Instead they became afraid and hid from God. They saw God as angry, severe—as an unwavering judge, not as the loving and compassionate Father that he is. Had they asked, they'd have been forgiven.

Fear is another consequence of Original Sin. How would you feel if you were separated from your parents and everyone who loves you? Most likely you'd be afraid and wonder *How will I survive? What's going to happen to me? What will I do next?* Without God's love and protection, we're afraid that we won't get what we need, that we aren't protected, that all will end badly.

change

Jesus Our Redeemer

Poor judgment is also a consequence of Original Sin. Whether you told a lie to avoid getting into trouble, yelled at your younger sister or brother, or took something that wasn't yours, you were using poor judgment. When you feel remorse or regret for acting unkindly toward others or doing something you know is unfair or unjust, it is because you are inherently good, but you used poor judgment. Because of Original Sin, we must fight the temptations that lead us to act wrongly.

The final consequence of Original Sin is death. When Adam and Eve disobeyed God, they experienced a spiritual death that led to physical death. Our physical lives decline, decay, and eventually end as well; death can be our greatest fear. But our spiritual lives can continue on with God in Heaven. Our hope is in God.

Original Sin puts us in a bad situation. We're a long way from home, separated from our Father, on our own in hostile country. Life is hard, and we make mistakes and do bad things. We wonder why it has to be this way. We always long for a better life.

If this were a movie, it would be time for the good guys to launch a rescue mission. In fact, that's what the Father did when he sent his Son, Jesus, to redeem us, but it's not a rescue mission from the movies. Jesus doesn't pluck us out of trouble and take us home, like a commando team whisking hostages to safety in a fleet of helicopters. Instead he opens up a way back home by fixing the problem that got us into trouble in the first place. Jesus does this by becoming human himself.

MY TURN: A Better Life

What good do you see happening in this world redeemed by a loving Jesus? Write your thoughts below.

_____

_____

_____

_____

_____

God Becomes Man

In Jesus, God became a human being and lived a fully human life. Everything you experience, he experienced too, except sin. Jesus had a childhood typical of his time. He knew what it was like to learn new things, to work hard, and to wish he were hanging out with his friends instead of finishing a job his mother gave him. As an adult he faced all the problems people today face. He knew fear, frustration, and the pain of family trouble. Jesus had friends betray him, and others ridicule and torture him. Jesus, the Son of God, was fully human.

One thing Jesus didn't experience was sin. Even though he faced temptations to sin, he didn't give in to them. Instead, he lived a life of perfect obedience to his Father, and he showed us how to do the same. Jesus is saying "I'm like you, so you can be like me."

The Great Reversal

Jesus completely reversed Adam and Eve's sin and its consequences. The Original Sin of Adam and Eve was an act of defiance. The Garden of Eden was the perfect place to be, but living there meant obeying God.

Adam and Eve disobeyed God; Jesus loved and obeyed his Father perfectly. We're consumed by love of money and material things; Jesus lived a life of poverty. We want power over others; Jesus spent his life serving. We want to be noticed and admired; Jesus was humble. We're afraid of many things; Jesus constantly said, "Fear not." At every step, Jesus overcame our sins and weaknesses.

The final consequence of Original Sin is death. Jesus accepted the terrible death inflicted by his enemies because it was his Father's will that he endure everything that human beings experience. But Jesus overcame death too. His Father raised him from the dead. The **Resurrection** of Jesus means that death is not the end for us. As Saint Paul wrote, "For just as in Adam all die, so too in Christ shall all be brought to life." (1 Corinthians 15:22)

SACRED SIGN: The Lamb of God

The lamb, a symbol of innocence, was often used in Old Testament times as a victim sacrificed to God for the sins of the people. Jesus was the innocent victim whose sacrificial death saved the people. This is why Jesus is called "the Lamb of God, who takes away the sin of the world." (John 1:29)

Salvation Today

God's rescue mission is still underway. Original Sin is still part of our lives. Jesus opened the way back to his Father's house, but each of us must choose to walk that path that leads us back home.

Jesus did several deeds to make sure that his work of **Salvation** continues. Here are four of the most important ones:

- **Served Others.** We learn how to act rightly by obeying Jesus' teaching and following his example. At his Last Supper with his disciples on the night before he died, Jesus summed up his teaching by washing his friends' feet. (John 13:1–17) This shocked the Apostles; washing people's feet was a job for the lowliest servant in the household. Jesus did it in order to show his friends—and us—that humble service to other people is the best way to live as his follower.

- **Instituted the Eucharist.** During the Last Supper, Jesus shared bread and wine with his Apostles, saying "[T]his is my body" and "[T]his is my blood . . ." (Matthew 26:26–28)

He told them to continue to do this as a memorial of his sacrifice. This sharing of the Body and Blood of Christ is central to every Mass. It is called the **Eucharist,** a word that means "thanksgiving," and it is a central way that Jesus Christ is present to us.

- **Established the Church.** After he rose from the dead, Jesus gave his Apostles the mission of continuing his work of Salvation. He said, "Go, therefore, and make disciples of all nations, baptizing them in the name of the Father, and of the Son, and of the holy Spirit, teaching them to observe all that I have commanded you. And behold, I am with you always, until the end of the age." (Matthew 28:19–20) The bishops of the Catholic Church are the successors of the Apostles. The Church baptizes people into the new life of Christ and teaches with his authority.

- **Sent the Holy Spirit.** Jesus sent the Holy Spirit to be with the human race until the end of time. The Holy Spirit is the active presence of God. The Spirit is the way God

RITE: Words of Absolution

In the Sacrament of Penance and Reconciliation, the priest absolves us with these words of the sins we confess:

God, the Father of mercies,
through the death and the resurrection
   of his Son
has reconciled the world to himself
and sent the Holy Spirit among us
for the forgiveness of sins;
through the ministry of the Church
may God give you pardon and peace,
and I absolve you from your sins
in the name of the Father, and of the Son,
   and of the Holy Spirit.

continues his work of saving and healing the world. Every Christian receives the Spirit. We can trust the Spirit to guide us as we love and serve God and other people.

The Cross Means Victory

Have you ever wondered why the cross is the symbol of Christianity? To many, the cross means pain and death; Jesus *died* on the cross. But for Christians, the cross means triumph and victory. It means that God has conquered death, and that there is always hope. It means that we can go where Jesus has gone—to the Father's house. That's why Christians proudly display the cross. It helps us see our lives united with Christ's life. The cross is the sign of God, who is love itself.

WITNESS: Saint Paul

Saul of Tarsus was a devout Jew who led the persecution of Christians in Jerusalem after Jesus' Death and Resurrection. Then Jesus appeared to Saul and called him to become an apostle of the new faith. Saul changed his name to Paul and became the greatest missionary of the early Church. Thirteen letters attributed to Paul are part of the New Testament.

MY TURN: Personal Symbols

In the space above, draw what your symbol would be to show that Christ is with you. On the lines below, explain why you chose your symbol.

_____

_____

_____

_____

summary

Words to Know

Eucharist   sin
Original Sin   Salvation
Resurrection

FAITH SUMMARY

God made humans without sin, but Adam and Eve disobeyed God and introduced Original Sin. Through his Salvation, Jesus reverses Original Sin. Jesus shows us how to walk the path that leads us back to God.

REMEMBER

What is Original Sin?

Original Sin is the condition of separation from God that all human beings suffer.

What are some of the consequences of Original Sin?

The consequences include a distorted idea of God, fear, unsound judgment, and death.

How did Jesus repair the damage done by Original Sin?

Jesus opened the way back to God by living a sinless life of perfect obedience to God. His Resurrection from the dead overcame death for all humankind.

How does the work of Salvation continue today?

Jesus' work of saving the world continues through service to others, the Eucharist, the Catholic Church, and the active presence of the Holy Spirit in our lives.

REACH OUT

1. Brainstorm four or five ways you can imitate Jesus and serve your community. Where is the greatest need? How can you help?

2. Pick one way to serve your community this week. Reflect on your experience in your personal journal. Remember that you will not be asked to share your responses.

REFLECT

Sometimes it is difficult to do what is right. Why do you think that is? Write about how you feel when you are cruel or mean-spirited and how you feel when you act kindly toward someone.

_____

_____

_____

_____

_____

_____

_____

_____

_____

_____

Thank you, Jesus, for loving and saving me. I want to be like you and love others as you did. Give me the grace to follow you. Amen.

One Body, One family

You are many things at once: a son or daughter, sibling, friend, classmate, teammate, athlete, student. Each of these titles means you belong to a community. What does belonging to these communities mean to you?

"In my Father's house there are many dwelling places. If there were not, would I have told you that I am going to prepare a place for you? And if I go and prepare a place for you, I will come back again and take you to myself, so that where I am you also may be." –*John 14:2–3*

What Is the Church?

The word *church* means many things: a building where we attend Mass, a religious service whereby we practice our faith, and the Roman Catholic organization under the leadership of the pope and the bishops. The Church includes all these things, but the heart of the Church that Jesus founded is something else. The word *Church* translates to "those who are called." The Christian Church is the people whom Christ has called to be with him personally. Scripture describes the Church in personal terms. It's a family, a people, the body of Christ.

The Four Marks

What is your family like? You might say things like, "We are loud," "We're outdoorsy," "Cooking together is our thing," or "We like puzzles." Let's ask the same thing about our family, the Church. What's the Church like? A good place to start is something we say every time we pray the Nicene Creed: "I believe in one, holy, catholic and apostolic Church." These four adjectives are called the four **Marks of the Church.** Just as your own family is not one adjective over another, the Church is not all one thing. The four Marks of the Church are the foundation from where we begin to recognize ourselves as Catholics.

The Church is a living body. The Church is the **People of God.** We're not saved as individuals; we're saved together, as the people whom God loves. Original Sin separated the whole human race from God. Jesus redeems the whole human race as a people.

The Church is also the **Body of Christ** on earth, bringing love and healing to the world. Jesus is the head; we are the hands and feet and eyes and ears and every other part of the body. The institutional Church is simply the way our family of faith is organized.

MY TURN: Let's Get Personal

List four ways that you spend time with other Catholics.

- _____
- _____
- _____
- _____

Which of these ways do you enjoy the most? Why?

_____

_____

Being a good Catholic isn't simply a matter of going to Mass more often or spending more time in church-related activities. God is present everywhere in the world—in your schoolwork, the places you go, your friends and family. There are many ways to love God. The key to being more spiritual is learning to recognize the presence of God in all things.

The Church Is One

There's only one Church because there's only one Christ. That means that the Body of Christ on earth is one body. There are more than a billion Catholics in the world. What does it mean to say that we're "one"? The epistle to the Ephesians puts it this way: "one Lord, one faith, one baptism; one God and Father of all, who is over all and through all and in all." (Ephesians 4:5–6) We're united in four ways.

- **One Baptism.** We're all baptized into new life in Christ in the name of the Father, and of the Son, and of the Holy Spirit.

- **One faith.** We believe the same things about God, Salvation, the Church, and the life to come. This is the faith received from the Apostles and summarized in the Nicene and Apostles' Creeds.

- **One worship.** We celebrate the same Mass and the same sacraments.

- **One government.** The Church is led by the bishops, the successors to the Apostles. The **pope** is the Bishop of Rome, who is successor to Peter and the head of the Apostles.

Sadly, the unity of Christians isn't perfect. The issues dividing Christians involve worship, church government, and beliefs. Orthodox and Protestant Christians, for example, do not accept the authority of the pope. Protestants differ from Catholics (and the Orthodox) in their view of the priesthood, worship and sacraments, and the role of Mary and the saints in the life of the Church. These divisions mean

Bamako cathedral, Catholic mass, Bamako, Mali, Africa.

that different church bodies are in different degrees of communion with the one Church. Catholics are in full communion.

Even though Christians are divided over important questions, there's a real unity among us. We're all baptized into the new life of Christ, and one Baptism joins us together into the one People of God, even if the unity is incomplete. All Christians believe that Jesus established one Church.

The Church Is Holy

Holy can mean perfect in goodness and righteousness. This brings up a good question: how can a Church full of sinners be "holy"? It's like a joke by the famous 20th-century comedian Groucho Marx: "I refuse to join any club that would have me for a member."

But the Church isn't a club. It's the People of God and the Body of Christ. The Church is holy because Christ is holy. The **Fathers of the Church,** the leaders of the Church in the

foundation

years after the Apostles, said that the Church is like the moon: all its light is reflected from the sun, and the sun is Christ. For us, holiness is something we're striving for. We grow in holiness when we act generously instead of selfishly, when we think of others instead of ourselves, when we do the right thing at home, in school, and with our friends. We're learning how to let the light of Christ shine in us.

The Church Is Catholic

You are a Catholic with a capital *C*, meaning a member of the worldwide Christian body that's in communion with the Bishop of Rome. The Catholic Church is also **catholic** with a lowercase *c*. By *catholic* we mean that the Church is "universal."

It's universal in extent, and we're not just talking geographically. Jesus told the Apostles to take the gospel to "all nations," and that's exactly what they did. People of every race, language, culture, and nation belong to the Catholic Church. The people you're part of include Indonesians, Nigerians, Swedes, Bolivians, Australians, Inuit, Spaniards, Pacific Islanders, and people from everywhere else on earth. This gives real meaning to the term *diversity.* Every culture and every sort of person has his or her home in the Church.

The Church is also universal in the sense that it contains everything that's needed for Salvation. The Gospel it preaches is good news for everyone. The faith it proclaims is the whole faith. Nothing essential is left out. Its mission is to all people everywhere and at all times.

Universality doesn't mean uniformity. Quite the opposite, in fact. For instance, Mass is celebrated in every language. Catholic life is as diverse as the people who live it.

MY TURN: People I Admire

Think of someone you admire. What do you like about this person? What characteristics does he or she have that you would like to have?

_____

_____

_____

_____

_____

The Church Is Apostolic

Apostolic refers to Jesus' twelve Apostles. The Church is apostolic because it was founded by Jesus and carried on by the Apostles. The Church holds to the Apostles' tradition and is governed by their successors, the bishops.

Jesus had a large circle of disciples around him, both men and women. From this group he selected twelve Apostles who had special responsibilities. These men, sometimes called the Twelve, went everywhere with Jesus and were eyewitnesses to his work. The Twelve were at the Last Supper, where Jesus gave them his Body and Blood and said, "[D]o this in memory of me." (Luke 22:19)

After his Resurrection, Jesus appeared to the Apostles and gave them the mission of continuing his work of preaching the gospel to the whole world through the Church he founded. When one died, the others chose his successor—a practice called apostolic succession that has continued through the centuries to the present day. The bishops of the Catholic Church are the direct successors to the twelve Apostles. They act with the same authority.

The pope and bishops may be direct successors of the Apostles, but there's a sense in which all of us are Apostles. The word *apostle* means "one who is sent out." All of us are sent to bring Christ's love to the world. In fact, this is the special responsibility of the **laity,** that is, Christians who are not ordained.

The Saints

You'll find saints everywhere in Catholic life. Parishes are named for saints. We have statues and pictures of saints. We tell stories from the lives of the saints. We say prayers asking saints to help us. You might even be named for a saint. When you're confirmed, you'll have the chance to take the name of a saint who will be your special patron. Why do we pay so much attention to saints anyway?

One reason is that the saints are just as relevant to our lives today as they were in their lifetime. The saints are a select group that have been **canonized;** that is, the Church has officially declared that they led especially holy lives. We are all called to be saints. Canonized saints show us that sanctity is something we can all achieve. The saints live with Christ in Heaven and are part of the same Church we belong to.

How the Saints Can Help

Think of the saints as friends who help us in several ways.

Saints are examples for us. They opened their hearts to God's grace and found a way to holiness. They faced real-life problems, had family troubles, were misunderstood, failed, and sinned. Sometimes people think that the saints are like comic-book superheroes— people with abilities far beyond our own. It's just the opposite: they are people like us who accomplished great things through God's grace. They show us that we can do the same.

SACRED SIGN: Scapular

A popular sacramental is the scapular, two small pieces of cloth attached to strings and worn around the neck so that one piece hangs in front and the other in back. It recalls the habits worn over the shoulders by members of religious orders. The two pieces of cloth show an image of Mary or a symbol of particular devotion. The Brown Scapular of Our Lady of Mount Carmel signifies the wearer's devotion to Mary, her motherly protection, and support of the Carmelite Order.

Madonna (love), 2010,
acrylic on canvas, Laura James.

know more than we do. When she was dying, Saint Thérèse of Lisieux said, "I want to spend my heaven in doing good on earth." The next time you need something, ask Saint Thérèse or another favorite saint to **intercede** with God on your behalf.

Saints bring us closer to Christ. We can look to the saints as examples of how to live Jesus' message—how the saints treated other people, how they handled conflict, how they made decisions. The lives of the saints point toward Jesus' way.

Mary

One saint in Heaven stands above all others—Mary, Jesus' mother. We revere her because she was closer to Jesus than any other person could ever be on this earth. Jesus honored her by taking her to Heaven, body and soul, to be with him.

Why Mary Is Special

It's easy to feel close to Mary. She's an ordinary woman, yet she became the Mother of God.

God invited Mary to become the mother of Jesus, but she didn't have to do it. She had a choice. Mary was confident that God would be with her so she said yes to his invitation. In this, Mary is our model. Jesus invites each of

Saints come in every size, shape, and race. Among them are teenagers, married people, monks, kings, soldiers, and school teachers. Saints come from every culture, continent, and century. Some were "saintly" from an early age; some were steadfast sinners who experienced a conversion. Some became famous; some were obscure. What each saint has in common is that each found his or her own way to be closer to God. You can be a saint in your own way too.

We can ask for the saints' help and guidance any time. They are part of our family of faith. They are closer to God than we are and they

RITE: Holy Water

The sprinkling of holy water recalls the Sacrament of Baptism. When we make the Sign of the Cross with holy water, we are praising the Trinity. The holy water in the baptismal font and in the receptacles at the church entryways are blessed during the Easter Vigil on Holy Saturday.

us to follow him. Doing this requires courage because we don't know what the future holds, but we can do it because we have confidence in God. Mary showed us how to say yes.

The Church believes that Mary, along with Jesus, was the only human being to be born free of Original Sin. God honored Mary in this special way to prepare her to become the mother of the Savior. This honor is known as the **Immaculate Conception.** Christians have believed in Mary's Immaculate Conception since the earliest days of the Church.

The Church believes that when her time on earth was complete, Mary was assumed into Heaven, body and soul, where she joined her Son, Jesus. This is called the **Assumption** of Mary. This is another unique privilege that God gave to Mary because of her role as the mother of the Savior.

The Church says that Mary is our mother as well as Jesus' mother. On the cross, Jesus pointed to Mary and said to his disciple John, "Behold, your mother." (John 19:27) The Church understands this to mean that Jesus entrusted the entire Church to Mary. Since we are the Church, Mary is our mother, and we can confidently call on her to intercede for us.

WITNESS: Venerable Pierre Toussaint

Venerable Pierre Toussaint was born in Haiti in 1766 and worked as a slave for a prominent family. When the family moved to New York, Pierre went with them and was made a hairdresser's apprentice. Pierre soon earned his freedom and his own money. He continued to care for the family he worked for when his master died. Pierre contributed all his money to several charities, including a Catholic orphanage. Pierre was known for his humility and compassion for all people, regardless of status.

MY TURN: Saintly Traits

List some of the qualities you think a saintly person would have.

_____

_____

_____

_____

summary

FAITH SUMMARY

The four Marks of the Church show us how the Church is one, holy, catholic, and apostolic. However, the Church is one community under God. We can learn how to live as part of this community through the examples of the saints. Mary, Jesus' mother, showed us how to say yes to Jesus and turn to God for guidance.

REMEMBER

What are the four Marks of the Church?

The Church is one, holy, catholic, and apostolic.

How is the Church one?

The Church has one baptism, one faith, one worship, and one government.

How can the saints help us?

We learn from the saints' example. They show us that there are many ways to holiness. They pray for us.

Why is Mary especially worthy of our devotion?

Mary shows us how to say yes and to follow Jesus in difficult circumstances. God preserved Mary from Original Sin. She is the mother of Jesus and the mother of God. When her time on earth was over, God assumed her into Heaven. She is the mother of the Church and the mother of every Christian.

REACH OUT

1. Research your patron saint or the saint on whose feast day you were born. What makes that saint holy?

2. Ask your friends and family about their favorite saints and why they like these saints.

REFLECT

As a Catholic, you belong to the community of the Church. What is expected of you, and what do you expect from the Church?

_____

_____

_____

_____

_____

_____

_____

_____

_____

Mary, my mother, I ask you to watch over me. Protect me. Pray for me. Remember me to your Son, Jesus. Thank you for your guidance. Amen.

Worshiping as a
community

Gestures, such as clapping or giving a thumbs-up, express a feeling without using words. What are some other gestures we use to communicate? How would you tell someone that you love them without using words?

For I received from the Lord what I also handed on to you, that the Lord Jesus, on the night he was handed over, took bread, and, after he had given thanks, broke it and said, "This is my body that is for you. Do this in remembrance of me." In the same way also the cup, after supper, saying, "This cup is the new covenant in my blood. Do this, as often as you drink it, in remembrance of me." For as often as you eat this bread and drink the cup, you proclaim the death of the Lord until he comes.
−1 Corinthians 11:23–26

God Lives Among Us

Sometimes it's easy to go to Mass. Sometimes it's not. You'd rather stay inside on a cold, wet winter morning or head to the pool on a summer Sunday. Going to Mass and offering worship takes time and effort, like everything else that's worth doing. Taking the time is a little easier if you make it a habit. It's also easier when you keep in mind that Catholic worship helps us realize how much Jesus is a part of our life.

Worship

In Hebrew, the word for *worship* (shachach) actually means "to bow before" in a posture of submission. To bow to someone or something is to physically orient or align ourselves with that person or thing. It is to say, in essence, "I direct all my being—physical, emotional, and spiritual—to you." This is why the First Commandment directs us not to bow before any false gods. God is telling us that when we align ourselves with someone or something other than him, we are not aligned with our true source. No doubt this is why the very first words of Jesus' public ministry were, "Repent, and believe in the gospel." (Mark 1:15) To repent is to reform or to start over again. It means to die to our old self—to die to sin—and to be reformed, born anew, in the grace of God. No longer are we to be aligned with sin, but rather we are to be aligned with the will of God.

Liturgy

As Catholics we believe certain things, but we also do certain things. Every Sunday, we gather for worship—something that Christians have been doing for nearly two thousand years. The surest way to declare our identity as a Catholic is to join our fellow Catholics at Mass on Sunday.

The word for public community worship is *liturgy,* from a Greek word meaning "work of the people." Liturgy is not something we do alone. It is something we do with or on behalf of the community of the faithful—the Church. Liturgy does not just refer to the celebration of the Mass, but to all the official public prayers of the Church. The Mass is the main form of liturgy, but there are others, most importantly the sacraments.

MY TURN: Speaking in Sign Language

What rituals do you have within your family? Pick one ritual and describe what it means to you and your family.

_____

_____

_____

_____

_____

Sunday—the Lord's Day

Jesus rose from the dead on a Sunday. Sunday immediately became the special day of the week when Christians gathered to pray and "to break bread." (Acts of the Apostles 20:7) This was the Eucharistic meal where Christians shared the bread and wine transformed into the Body and Blood of Christ. Ever since, Sunday has been the day of the week set aside for the principal celebration of the Eucharist.

Sacraments

When we celebrate the sacraments, we are signaling to God and to the community that we are strengthening our relationship with God and actively participating in our spiritual education.

The sacraments are sacred signs that bring God's love and grace to us through familiar things. There are seven sacraments; the most important one is the Eucharist, which is celebrated at every Mass. The Eucharist and the six other sacraments are central to the Church's liturgical life. Each of them brings us God's grace through a sacred sign.

How Sacraments Work

The visible signs of these sacraments convey an invisible reality—God's love and grace and blessing for our lives. It's like a hug. A hug is something you do. It's a visible sign of the invisible love you have for the person you're hugging. The visible hug and the invisible love can't be separated. You hug someone because you love them; by hugging them, you're giving them love. The same idea is at work in the sacraments. New life in Christ comes through the water of Baptism. Jesus gives to us the consecrated bread and wine, his Body and Blood.

Sacraments make things concrete. Being a Christian isn't a set of ideas and beliefs in our heads. God's love isn't merely an invisible "spiritual" reality. Our love of God isn't just words. The first followers of Jesus touched him, heard him, walked with him. We can do the same through the sacraments. The sacraments let us love God with all our senses, not just with our minds.

Sacraments of Initiation

Three of the sacraments are called Sacraments of Initiation because they make us full members of the Church. You may have gone through initiation rituals in organizations like the Scouts, athletic teams, and clubs. You're fully part of the Catholic Church when you receive the sacraments of Baptism, Confirmation, and the Eucharist.

In **Baptism,** we come into a new life in Christ. We are baptized "In the name of the Father, and of the Son, and of the Holy Spirit." Baptism's primary symbol is water—a necessity for the life and growth of living things.

The **Eucharist,** the most important sacrament of all, brings us Christ himself through the signs of bread and wine.

Confirmation completes our initiation into the Church. You are anointed with holy oil, an ancient symbol signifying special attachment to a group.

believe

Sacraments of Healing

The two Sacraments of Healing restore us to spiritual and sometimes physical health.

In the Sacrament of **Penance and Reconciliation,** we confess our sins and receive God's forgiveness. The grace of the sacrament comes through words— we name our sins, and the priest gives God's forgiveness through words of absolution.

The Anointing of the Sick brings comfort and sometimes healing to those suffering from physical, spiritual, and emotional illness. The sacrament uses oil, an ancient sign of healing.

Sacraments of Service

Two sacraments give special graces of service.

In **Matrimony,** a man and a woman commit themselves to love and care for each other for the rest of their lives. The grace of the sacrament comes through the vows that the man and woman say to each other. They also usually exchange rings as a sign of love and fidelity.

Through the Sacrament of **Holy Orders,** men are ordained to serve the Church as priests. A key moment in this sacrament occurs when the bishop lays hands on the man and says the words of ordination. The laying on of hands is an ancient sign of affection, healing, and special anointing for service.

MY TURN: Favorite Things

What objects are special signs to you? Perhaps they symbolize or remind you of important people or events in your life. List three of them and explain why they are sacred to you.

_____

_____

_____

_____

_____

The Liturgical Year

Catholic worship has a pattern too. It happens in an annual cycle of seasons and feasts called the liturgical year, also called the Church year and the Christian year.

The liturgical year is divided into seasons, each with its own traditions and ways of praying.

It begins with Advent, which starts on the fourth Sunday before Christmas and ends on Christmas Eve. The theme of Advent is waiting. We wait for two events: the birth of Jesus at Christmas, and the second coming of Christ at the end of time. Advent is observed by special Scripture readings at Mass.

The Christmas season celebrates the birth of Jesus and his becoming known to the world. It begins on the evening of Christmas Eve and continues through the Feast of the Baptism of the Lord, celebrated on the Sunday after January 6.

Lent is a solemn time of prayer and reflection that leads up to Easter. It begins on Ash Wednesday, six weeks before Easter, and lasts for 40 days (Sundays in Lent are not counted). Catholics typically observe Lent by fasting, spending more time in prayer, and helping those in need.

The week before Easter is called Holy Week and is a time of special prayer and worship services recalling the Passion, Death, and Resurrection of Jesus. It begins on Palm Sunday, named for the palms waved by the crowds celebrating Jesus' arrival in Jerusalem the week of his death. Masses on Holy Thursday mark Jesus' Last Supper and his celebration of the first Eucharist. A special service on Good Friday afternoon observes the Death of Jesus. Easter is the celebration of his Resurrection from the dead. The Easter season ends with the Feast of Pentecost, marking the coming of the Holy Spirit to the Church.

The rest of the liturgical year is called Ordinary Time. The first block of Ordinary Time is the time between the Christmas season and Lent. The second part is the weeks after Pentecost until the beginning of Advent.

SACRED SIGN: Incense

During the Easter season and at other special times, the priest and people are blessed at Mass with incense, a sweet-smelling smoke. The incense is thrown onto burning coals in a container called a thurible. The smoke of burning incense symbolizes the prayers of the people rising to Heaven. "Let my prayer be incense before you." (Psalm 141:2)

Celebrating the Paschal Mystery

Through the liturgical year and the sacraments, we celebrate the **Paschal Mystery**. In biblical tradition, a mystery is not something to be solved, but something to be entered into and to stand in awe of. In essence, a mystery is something that is revealed and yet remains hidden. Even though God has revealed himself to us throughout all of Salvation history, culminating in the pinnacle of his Revelation, Jesus Christ, God remains beyond our grasp. We can encounter God. We can know God. But we cannot solve God. When we Catholics hear about the mystery of our faith, the Paschal Mystery of Jesus, the mystery of the Trinity, or the mysteries of the Rosary, we might wonder how we are supposed to solve all these mysteries.

Sacred Signs

Language alone fails us when trying to explain the mystery of God. As Catholics, we rely on signs, symbols, rituals, and gestures to express our encounters with God. A common question might be *"Where do I find God?"* Catholic worship strongly emphasizes God's presence in the world that we experience every day. God is here. We can experience him in things that we touch, see, hear, feel, and taste. We worship in churches adorned with statues, stained-glass windows, flowers, and crosses. The priest wears colorful **vestments** and uses beautiful vessels on the altar. We sing sacred music. On special occasions, **incense** is used to bless the altar and the people.

RITE: Proclaiming the Word of God

The celebration of all the sacraments includes the proclamation of God's Word as found in the Bible. It is in this Word that we find the fullness of God's Revelation. When we listen carefully with open hearts, God invites us into a deeper relationship with him.

Sacramentals

The objects that are part of Catholic devotion are known as **sacramentals.** They include religious medals, rosaries, holy water, crucifixes, holy oil, candles, and bells. We observe Advent with an Advent wreath and Christmas with a Nativity scene. We receive ashes on Ash Wednesday and palms on Palm Sunday. Sacramentals also include gestures. We make the Sign of the Cross, we genuflect in church, and we sometimes kneel when we pray.

Sacramentals are "sign language"—a way of communicating without words. We communicate in sign language all the time. You can express yourself or communicate an emotion by the jewelry you wear, the way you decorate your room, your user name, and your social-networking profile. A gift of red roses says something. So does a wedding ring. So does putting your arm around the shoulder of a friend who is upset. These signs and symbols often speak more powerfully than words— sometimes much more powerfully.

God uses sign language to communicate his love and grace to us. While the most powerful of these signs are the sacraments, sacramentals also enrich our understanding of and devotion to God.

WITNESS: Saint Pius X

Giuseppe Melchiorre Sarto was born in Italy in 1835. He became a priest when he was 23 years old. When he became pope, he changed his name to Pius X and instituted changes regarding children and the Eucharist. Children began receiving Holy Communion not long after they reached the age of discretion, which was age seven. The changes he instituted are still observed today.

MY TURN: This is the Day the Lord Has Made

Every day is a gift from God. Reflect on and then write five things you are grateful for this day.

_____

_____

_____

_____

_____

summary

FAITH SUMMARY

The Mass is a central part of the way we as Catholics thank and praise Jesus and strengthen our relationship with God. We are nourished by Jesus' sacrifice in the Eucharist. Just as we express our love for friends and families through words and gestures, we express our love for God through sacraments and worship.

REMEMBER

What is the liturgical year?
The liturgical year is the annual cycle of Christian worship. Its principal seasons are Advent, Christmas, Lent, and Easter. The time between seasons is called Ordinary Time.

What are the three types of sacraments?
Sacraments of Initiation (Baptism, Confirmation, and Eucharist), Sacraments of Healing (Penance and Reconciliation, Anointing of the Sick), and Sacraments of Service (Matrimony and Holy Orders)

What is the Paschal Mystery?
The Paschal Mystery is the suffering, Death, Resurrection, and Ascension of Jesus—the sacrifice by which we are freed from the bondage of sin.

What are sacramentals? Give examples of sacramentals.
Sacramentals are the objects that are part of Catholic devotion. Some examples of sacramentals are the rosary, incense, vestments, hymns, and oil.

REACH OUT

1. Ask your friends to tell you about sacred objects that they find meaningful, such as religious medals, holy pictures, and songs.

2. Join an activity in your parish that serves the community, such as reading or singing at Mass.

REFLECT

Mass is a time for both personal communication with God and worship as a community of believers. Write about why you think both aspects of Mass are important to the Catholic faith.

_____

_____

_____

_____

_____

_____

O my God, I love you above all things with my whole heart and soul because you are good and worthy of all my love. I love my neighbor as myself for the love of you. I forgive all who have injured me and I ask pardon of those whom I have injured. Amen.

Welcome, Strength, and
nourishment

Recall times when you were preparing to go away on a trip. How did you feel? Excited? Anxious? Both?

Did you get to your destination and discover that you forgot to pack something important? What did you do about it?

[T]hey asked Peter and the other apostles, "What are we to do, my brothers?" Peter [said] to them, "Repent and be baptized, every one of you, in the name of Jesus Christ for the forgiveness of your sins; and you will receive the gift of the holy Spirit."   –*Acts of the Apostles 2:37–38*

Planting Your Roots

You've probably heard someone compare life to a journey. Maybe you've heard this more than once. It's a common analogy that happens to fit pretty well. Your life *is* a journey. You don't know where it will take you, but it's sure to contain adventures, challenges, surprises, disappointments, and triumphs. You've experienced some of these already. There are more to come.

Your main job right now is to get ready for the journey. You're getting an education, developing your talents, acquiring skills, making friends, and learning how to deal with challenges and surprises. Getting ready includes laying a solid spiritual foundation. Three sacraments of the Catholic Church help you do this: Baptism, Confirmation, and the Eucharist. They connect you with God by firmly planting you in Christ's Church and giving you strength and food for the journey.

Sacraments of Initiation

Many organizations and clubs have a procedure to bring in new members. Often a ritual is involved. Public officials begin their work by taking an oath of office. A new principal might be formally introduced at a school assembly.

These are rites of initiation—something we do at the beginning of things. For Catholics, Baptism, Confirmation, and the Eucharist are the **Sacraments of Initiation.** When you receive them, you're fully Catholic. You are just as much a Catholic as the pope is.

Initiation into the spiritual life is like the beginning of our natural lives. We are born, strengthened, and fed. In Baptism we are born into the new life in Christ. Confirmation strengthens us with the Gifts of the Holy Spirit. The Eucharist gives us the food that's essential to the spiritual life. In the Catholic Church, these three sacraments are usually given in the first 10 to 15 years of life. The Sacraments of Initiation go together even though they're received at different times.

MY TURN: Part of the Group

Remember a time when you came into a new group—a new school, a club, a sports team, a circle of friends. What happened to make you feel as if you belonged?

_____

_____

_____

_____

_____

Baptism

Every Christian is baptized. When people asked the first Christians in Jerusalem what they needed to do to be saved, Peter answered "Repent and be baptized, every one of you, in the name of Jesus Christ." (Acts of the Apostles 2:38) Baptism is necessary. Baptism frees us from sin and makes us sons and daughters of God. We are incorporated into the Church and made part of the Church's mission.

Reading the Signs of Baptism

Words can't adequately describe what Baptism does, so we Catholics turn to comparisons, analogies, images, and signs. The primary sign is water. The word *baptism* comes from a Greek word meaning to "plunge or immerse in water." Water is essential for life. We, who can turn on a faucet anytime we need water, tend to forget this. The Jews and Christians in Palestine who spent a lot of time in the desert never forgot that. For them, water was quite literally the source of life. That's why the Bible is full of images of life-giving water springing up from the earth.

Water means both life and death in Baptism. Symbolically, the sinful person is plunged into water and "dies," then is pulled out of the water and "born again." Today most infants and adults are baptized by having water poured over their heads, but the rite still signifies dying and being born again.

The Rite of Baptism

The Sign of the Cross. Like Mass and other liturgies, Baptism begins with the Sign of the Cross: "In the name of the Father, and of the Son, and of the Holy Spirit."

Scripture readings. The Gospel is proclaimed through reading the written Word of God.

Anointing. The minister of Baptism drives away Satan and other evil spirits by anointing the person with oil.

Blessing the baptismal water. The priest blesses the water that will be used for Baptism.

Baptismal promises. The person (or the infant's parents and godparents) renounces Satan and professes the Christian faith.

The Rite of Baptism. The minister pours water three times over the person's head, saying "I baptize you in the name of the Father, and of the Son, and of the Holy Spirit." This is called the essential Rite of Baptism—the one part that's necessary for the person to be baptized.

Second anointing. The newly baptized Christian is anointed with oil again, a sacred sign of belonging to Christ.

White garment. The new Christian is wrapped in a white mantle or garment to symbolize "putting on Christ."

Candle. A candle is given to the new Christian symbolizing both Christ as "the light of the world" and our mission to bring light to the world.

Baptismal Promises

The **baptismal promises** are a series of questions that the minister of the sacrament asks the person seeking Baptism. If you were baptized as an infant, your parents and godparents answered these questions for you.

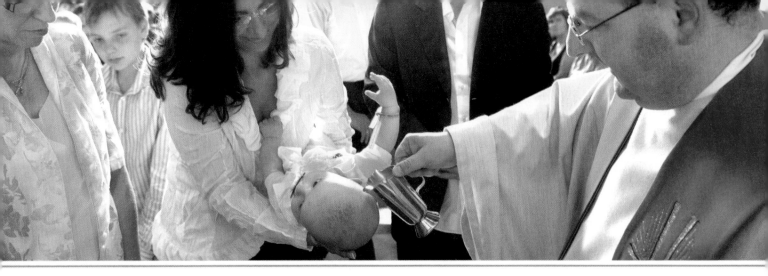

Who Is Baptized?

The Church now baptizes infants so that the family and the local Christian community can provide spiritual formation as early as possible. The baptismal ceremony also includes **godparents** who agree to help the parents with the spiritual development of the child. Baptism isn't a solitary sacrament. Infants are baptized into a community of faith.

Unbaptized adults come into the Church through a process called the **Rite of Christian Initiation of Adults (RCIA),** which is modeled closely on the ancient practices of the early Church. After months of instruction and formation, catechumens who have gone through the process are baptized at the Easter Vigil service. Adults who have been baptized in another Christian tradition join the Church by making a profession of faith and celebrating the Sacraments of Confirmation and the Eucharist. This is sometimes done during the Easter Vigil Service as well.

Confirmation

Baptism gets you started, but there's a whole life full of challenges ahead of you. Confirmation is the sacrament that gives you the knowledge, strength, insight, and grace to meet them. It brings the Gift of the Holy Spirit—the power of God and the constant presence of Jesus Christ in your life. The Holy Spirit comes to each of us in the Sacrament of Confirmation.

MY TURN: Signs

Write four ideas that you want to communicate to a friend. Examples: "You are special." "I need help." "I'm worried." Invent and describe signs to communicate these ideas without using words.

_____

_____

_____

_____

Reading the Signs of Confirmation

Oil. The word *Christian* comes from Greek words meaning "anointed." We were anointed with oil in Baptism. We're anointed again in Confirmation, and this time the oil has several meanings. It's a sign of abundance and joy, of cleansing and healing. All these come to us through the Holy Spirit. The special oil used at Confirmation is called Chrism, a perfumed oil.

Laying on of hands. Laying hands on another person is an ancient sign of blessing and healing. The apostles did it often after **Pentecost:** "they laid hands on them and they received the holy Spirit." (Acts of the Apostles 8:17) The same thing happens to you at Confirmation when the bishop lays a hand on your head.

Seal. A seal is a sign often meaning authority and ownership. Official documents are stamped with a seal. The brand on a rancher's cattle is a seal. The Christian meaning of the word comes from the seals that kings and high officials used to show that something

belongs to them. This is what Paul meant when he wrote that God has "put his seal upon us and given the Spirit in our hearts as a first installment." (2 Corinthians 1:22) When the bishop says "be sealed with the Gift of the Holy Spirit" at Confirmation, he means that you belong to Christ.

The Eucharist

The Eucharist completes the process of Catholic initiation. Baptism makes you a Christian. You get started on the journey of life—often literally so because most Catholics are baptized soon after they are born. Confirmation gives you strength for the journey; God will be with you through the power of the Holy Spirit. The Eucharist is food for the journey. All your life, Jesus is with you in the most intimate way.

Reading the Signs of the Eucharist

Bread and Wine. Bread is a symbol of life. Wine is a symbol of joy and abundance. It's easy to understand these signs. Bread, which sustains life, is also a symbol of the physical body, and red wine is a symbol of blood. That is the meaning of the bread and wine Jesus gave to his disciples at the Last Supper. He gave life and joy; he also gave his actual Body and Blood.

A Sacrifice. A sacrifice means giving up something good in order to have something better. You sacrifice time with your friends in order to study. You work hard practicing a musical instrument so that you can play it well.

SACRED SIGN: Oil

Holy oils are used in the Sacraments of Baptism, Confirmation, Holy Orders, and Anointing of the Sick. Traditionally, the bishop blesses the oils during Mass on Holy Thursday at the cathedral. The oils are Chrism, which is used in Baptism, Confirmation, and Holy Orders; oil of catechumens, which is used to anoint those joining the Church; and oil of the sick, which is used for Anointing of the Sick. Among the holy oils, only Chrism includes balm, which gives the oil its unique fragrance.

The Eucharist is a sacrifice too. The bread and wine offered at Mass belong to us. The liturgy calls them "the work of human hands." They are basic human food. The priest offers them to God. God returns the bread and wine to us as the Body and Blood of Christ—the gift of Jesus himself.

The Eucharistic sacrifice is a reenactment of Jesus' sacrifice on the Cross to restore humanity to friendship with God. It's the Paschal Mystery—the most important thing that has ever happened. It's something we experience every time we go to Mass.

A Meal. At its simplest, the Eucharist is a meal. We get together with people around a table, spend time together, and eat some food.

Meals are for groups of people. You don't usually call it a meal when you eat alone. The group we share the Eucharistic meal with is the local community of Catholics, which usually includes people we know. The table we gather around is the altar. We listen to stories about our family (the Scripture readings). We remember and honor our leader (Jesus). We pray together and sing songs. Then we eat his Body and drink his Blood. The food is Jesus Christ himself, given to us in the most intimate way. It is spiritual food. It's the nourishment we need to become the people we were meant to be.

The Real Presence

Jesus is present in a unique way in the Eucharist. The bread and wine of the Eucharist truly become the Body and Blood of Christ. This is called the **Real Presence.** It simply means that Jesus Christ is truly present in the Eucharist in a deeper way than in the other sacraments.

It's easier to receive the Gift of the Real Presence than it is to explain it. Jesus certainly intended that we should have him fully in the consecrated Bread and Wine of the Eucharist. How this comes about is something we can only partially understand. Speaking of the Eucharist, a great Father of the Church named Cyril said "Do not doubt whether this is true, but rather receive the words of the Savior in faith, for since he is the truth, he cannot lie."

RITE: Words of Consecration

The most solemn part of the Mass is found in the words of consecration. As the priest speaks these words, the bread and wine truly become the Body and Blood of Christ.

Take this, all of you, and eat of it,
for this is my Body,
which will be given up for you.
Take this, all of you, and drink from it,
for this is the chalice of my Blood,
the Blood of the new and eternal covenant,
which will be poured out for you and for many
for the forgiveness of sins.
Do this in memory of me.

Parts of the Mass

The Mass is the high point of the Catholic life, and it always follows a set order. It is an action of Christ and his Church that memorializes the Last Supper at which Jesus shared his Body and his Blood with his disciples.

There are five main parts of the Mass.

- **Introductory Rites**—We prepare to celebrate the Eucharist.

- **Liturgy of the Word**—We hear from the Bible the story of God's plan for Salvation.

- **Liturgy of the Eucharist**—We celebrate Christ's presence in the Eucharist.

- **Communion Rite**—We receive the Body and Blood of Jesus Christ.

- **Concluding Rites**—We are blessed and sent forth to live the Gospel.

People all over the world gather at God's Eucharistic table as brothers and sisters. The community is nourished by the Body and Blood of Christ and is sent into the world to serve God and to carry out the mission of the Church.

WITNESS: Saint Mary McKillop

Saint Mary McKillop (1842–1909) founded the Josephite order of nuns to work with those who are poor. She faced tremendous opposition to her work, much of it coming from priests and bishops. She overcame the obstacles by combining respect and obedience with a forceful defense of her ideas.

MY TURN: Personal Slogan

What phrase or short sentence would best describe you at this moment in your life? On the lines below, write two or three personal slogans that express who you are.

_____

_____

_____

_____

summary

FAITH SUMMARY

Baptism, Confirmation, and the Eucharist are the sacraments that establish us in the Christian life. Baptism frees us from Original Sin and makes us part of the Church. Confirmation strengthens us by giving us the Gifts of the Holy Spirit. In the Eucharist we receive the Body and Blood of Christ—spiritual food to nourish us.

REMEMBER

What are the Sacraments of Initiation?
Baptism, Confirmation, and the Eucharist.

What is the primary sign of Baptism, and what does it mean?
The primary sign is water. In ritual language, the person is symbolically plunged into water and pulled out, symbolizing dying and rising again to new life.

What does the bishop mean when he says, "Be sealed with the Gift of the Holy Spirit."
The Gift of the Holy Spirit in Confirmation is a seal—a sign that we belong to Christ.

What does the Church mean by the Real Presence of Christ in the Eucharist?
The Real Presence means that Christ is fully and completely present in the consecrated Bread and Wine which truly become his Body and Blood.

REACH OUT

1. Think of people in your community who are in need of help. Resolve to do something to reach out to them.

2. Where do you most need help in your life right now? When you get some time alone, ask Jesus to help you with this.

Words to Know

baptismal promises
godparents
Pentecost
Real Presence
Rite of Christian Initiation of Adults (RCIA)
Sacraments of Initiation

REFLECT

Think about this past week. List one example where you felt God's presence in your life. Describe your experience.

_____

_____

_____

_____

_____

_____

_____

_____

_____

Jesus, thank you for coming to me in the sacraments. Thank you for my family and friends and all the good things I have. I pray that you will always be with me and with those I love. Amen.

Forgiveness and
discipleship

Remember times when you were sick. How did people treat you? What made you feel better? What didn't help? Think of a time when someone you love was sick or not feeling well in body or heart. What did you do to help him or her?

The Pharisees and their scribes complained to his disciples, saying, "Why do you eat and drink with tax collectors and sinners?" Jesus said to them in reply, "Those who are healthy do not need a physician, but the sick do. I have not come to call the righteous to repentance but sinners."

–Luke 5:30–32

Help Along the Way

Baptism, Confirmation, and the Eucharist get you started. Baptism makes you a Christian, Confirmation gives you the Holy Spirit, and the Eucharist gives you Jesus Christ himself. You're ready! The other four sacraments might be called sacraments for living whole and fruitful lives. When you get into spiritual trouble, the Sacrament of Penance and Reconciliation sets things right again. Another Sacrament of Healing, the Sacrament of Anointing of the Sick, brings spiritual health—and often physical healing—to those who are ill. Two more sacraments—Matrimony and Holy Orders—equip Catholics for lives of service. A man and a woman permanently commit themselves to each other in marriage in the Sacrament of Matrimony. Holy Orders is the sacrament by which men are ordained as bishops, priests, and deacons.

Sacraments of Healing

During his time on earth, Jesus spent much of his time with those whom people might politely call "riffraff"—beggars, the disabled and seriously ill, poor people, children, and public sinners. He directed his teaching to them. He talked with them. He ate with them. This shocked the religious leaders of his time and they challenged him angrily: "Why do you eat and drink with tax collectors and sinners?" Jesus replied, "Those who are healthy do not need a physician, but the sick do." (Luke 5:30–31)

Those who are sick in body and spirit are Jesus' special friends. He loved them during his life on earth, and he loves them still. We are all broken or sick or not whole, and God loves us too. His special way of coming to us in our brokenness today is in the two Sacraments of Healing—Reconciliation and the Anointing of the Sick.

MY TURN: Healing Words

List words or phrases that immediately come to mind when you think of healing. Pick one word or phrase and explain the association.

_____

_____

_____

_____

_____

_____

Penance and Reconciliation

When you lash out at a friend in anger, you damage that friendship. When you envy someone or steal something, you retreat into a gloomy world of your own. When you lie or nurse resentments or break promises, you fail to be the person God created you to be. Sin separates us from God and from one another. Sin wrecks relationships. The Sacrament of Reconciliation puts things right. It restores our relationships and heals what's broken. *Reconciliation* means "to bring together, to meet again." We often lose our way. This sacrament is the way back home.

Opening this way back home was the first thing Jesus did after his Resurrection. He gathered the Apostles together and gave them the authority to forgive sins: "Receive the holy Spirit. Whose sins you forgive are forgiven them; and whose sins you retain, are retained." (John 20:22–23) Confession was a feature of the life of the early Church. It was often a public ritual, especially for serious and public sins. But by the early Middle Ages, the sacrament had taken the form it has today—primarily a private exchange between a **penitent** and a priest.

Reading the Signs of Reconciliation

Confession is the term commonly used for this sacrament, but the confession of one's sins to a priest is only one part of the sacrament. The other two parts are **contrition** and **penance.**

- **Contrition.** The process begins with contrition—the admission that we've done wrong, that we're responsible for the wrongdoing, and that we're sorry. Being honest about what we've done isn't always easy. Being reconciled begins with a frank admission that we've done wrong.

- **Confession.** The second part of the sacrament is confession. We confess our sins to a priest, and the priest speaks the words of absolution through which God forgives and pardons us.

- **Penance.** The final part of the sacrament is the penance. Usually the priest will ask us to say prayers or perform an act of charity. Through the penance we express our resolve to make things right. The penance is a reminder of the need to live differently, in accordance with God's will in us.

The Rite of Reconciliation

There is an order to the Sacrament of Reconciliation because it is a ritual, like the Mass and the other sacraments.

- We think about how we have sinned or wronged God or another person.

- We name the sin. Naming the sin is accepting that we have done wrong.

- The priest listens. In the Sacrament of Reconciliation, the priest is bound to absolute secrecy in order to preserve the dignity of the confessor. This secrecy is called the "sacramental seal."

- The priest suggests a fitting penance for us to receive forgiveness fully.

- We accept the penance and pray the Act of Contrition.

- The priest speaks the words of absolution. Our sins are forgiven, and we are dismissed to perform our penance.

healing

The Anointing of the Sick

Think of the last time you were sick; maybe you had the flu. Along with fever, cough, aches and pains can come gloominess, boredom, fatigue, and restlessness. Physical illness affects the emotions and spirit as well as the body.

Illness is both a spiritual opportunity and a spiritual challenge. It reminds us of something that's easy to forget when we're well: Our true strength comes from God alone. One of the reasons Jesus spent so much time with sinners, poor people, and sick people is that they understood how much they needed God. Sickness works the same way with us. When we're sick, our bodies and spirits are troubled. The Sacrament of the Anointing of the Sick is an encounter with Jesus Christ when we are in need of him.

Reading the Signs of the Anointing of the Sick

We usually *do* something to show love and support for a sick person—give him or her a hug, send a card, bring flowers or candy, sign the cast on a broken leg. The grace of the Sacrament of the Anointing of the Sick, as for all the sacraments, also comes through something tangible. The central sign is anointing the forehead and hands with holy oil.

Oil has several meanings in the Anointing of the Sick. As in other sacraments, using oil means being chosen and set apart. Oil is a seal—a sign of belonging to God and a sign of strength. Oil is also an ancient sign of healing. The sick person who is anointed receives all these graces: new life in Christ, strength as a member of Jesus' body, and healing of spirit and body.

The Church emphasizes the communal dimension of the sacrament. Family and friends are encouraged to be present for the sacrament. In many parishes today, the sacrament is given to many people at once in communal healing services.

MY TURN: The Best Medicine

When we are feeling down or sick, certain people or things always make us feel better. List some of the people or things that lift your spirits when you are ill or upset.

_____

_____

_____

Write a brief prayer of thanks for those people and things in your life that cheer you up.

_____

_____

_____

The Rite of Anointing of the Sick

Like other sacraments, the Anointing of the Sick follows a specific rite, or formal ceremonial act, that includes the following:

- A **Penitential Rite** where the sick person and others present ask God's forgiveness for sin.

- Readings from Scripture appropriate for this sacrament.

- The laying on of hands, an ancient sign of healing and blessing. The priest lays his hands on the sick person and prays.

- Anointing with oil. The priest says, "Through this holy anointing may the Lord in his love and mercy help you with the grace of the Holy Spirit. May the Lord who frees you from sin save you and raise you up."

- Participation in the Sacrament of Reconciliation.

- Reception of the Eucharist. The Eucharist is often given, especially to people who are near death. This final Eucharist is called **viaticum,** meaning "food for the journey."

The sacrament can be received more than once. Catholics need only to be suffering from a serious illness or medical condition.

Sacraments of Service

Matrimony and Holy Orders are sacraments that equip Catholics for work in the world. They are called Sacraments of Service because they prepare us to work for the good of others. In marriage, a man and a woman commit themselves to each other in a lifelong union of love and mutual help. In Holy Orders, men are ordained for lives of service to the Church. Both sacraments testify to one of the great secrets of a successful life: We are happiest when we serve others. As Saint Teresa of Ávila said, "Christ has no hands but ours to do his work today."

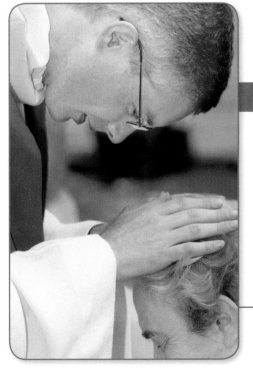

SACRED SIGN: Laying On of Hands

Laying on of hands is part of the rituals of the Sacraments of Baptism, Confirmation, Anointing of the Sick, and Holy Orders. In Holy Orders, it is the means by which a man is included in one of the orders of bishop, priest, or deacon. It signifies the passing on of the authority of the Apostles through apostolic succession. In the Sacrament of the Anointing of the Sick, it is a sign of the coming of the Holy Spirit to heal and strengthen the person who is ill.

Matrimony

Marriage shows us something of what God is like. God is a Trinity of three Persons joined in a union of love; a Christian marriage is a union of a man and a woman in a lifelong loving partnership. Marriage is like the Church in that the family is a society of people who love each other and work for each other's good.

A man and a woman begin their life together with a solemn promise to love and care for each other exclusively for the rest of their lives. In so doing, they receive the grace and strength they need to be faithful to this promise.

Reading the Signs of Matrimony

Marriage is unique in that the man and woman confer the sacrament on each other. The core of the Sacrament of Matrimony is the solemn promise of mutual love and fidelity. The Church cannot make this promise; only the man and woman entering into marriage can make it. The central part of this sacrament is the promise the bride and groom make to each other— the vows of Matrimony. Three elements are essential in these promises:

- The bride and groom cannot be forced to marry. They enter marriage by their own free choice. This is called free consent.

- The promise is for life, and it excludes other people.

- The couple promises to be open to the children that God might send and to raise them in the Church.

The Rite of Matrimony

The Rite of Matrimony for Catholic couples consists of the following essential elements:

- The minister invites the couple to offer their consent.

- The couple then publicly profess their consent, which is further symbolized by the blessing and exchanging of rings.

Holy Orders

In one sense, every Christian is a priest through Baptism. Ordained priests, bishops, and deacons are called in a special way. They bring God's love and grace as Christ's servants for the Church.

RITE: The Exchange of Rings

Before the vows, the priest or deacon presiding at the ceremony questions the couple about their intentions. He asks if they have come freely and without reservation. He asks, "Will you love and honor each other for the rest of your lives?" He asks if they are willing to accept children lovingly from God. After they answer yes to these questions, the bride and groom exchange rings and mutually promise "to be true in good times and in bad, in sickness and in health." They promise to love and honor each other all the days of their lives.

Reading the Signs of Holy Orders

Service is at the heart of all ordained ministry. Bishops, priests, and deacons represent Christ among us. One of the most important ways they do this is to imitate Christ as the humble servant, giving everything he has for the people he loves. The Sacrament of Ordination is called Holy Orders. It is plural because the Church is served by three orders.

- Bishops are the successors of the Apostles. Together with the Pope, the Bishop of Rome, they share responsibility for the apostolic mission of the entire Church.

- Priests are coworkers of the bishops. They act with the bishop's authority and exercise his pastoral ministry in many ways.

- Deacons are ordained to a ministry of service. They assist parish pastors in preaching, baptizing, witnessing at weddings, and assisting in Mass.

The Rite of Ordination

The Rites of Ordination for bishops, priests, and deacons consists of these essential elements:

- The bishop imposes his hands on those being ordained.

- The bishop says the words of consecration asking God to pour forth the Holy Spirit upon those being ordained.

- Bishops and priests are anointed with oil.

WITNESS: Saint Augustine

When Augustine was a young boy, he and his friends stole pears from a tree just to do something that wasn't allowed. Augustine felt shame for being so disrespectful and found redemption in the Catholic faith. At the age of 32, Augustine was baptized a Christian. He thought that he would live as a monk. However, the people of the town of Hippo in North Africa asked him to be their bishop. As bishop he preached and helped his people. He helped Catholics of his time and of every century since then to understand how much God—as Father, Son, and Holy Spirit—loves them. Augustine was named a Doctor of the Church, which means that the Church believes his insights and writings are essential contributions to Church teachings, such as Original Sin, free will, and the Trinity.

MY TURN: Called to Serve

Priests are called to serve God's people. List some ways you can serve God through your own parish.

_____

_____

_____

summary

FAITH SUMMARY

Reconciliation and the Anointing of the Sick are Sacraments of Healing that restore us to spiritual and often physical health. Matrimony and Holy Orders are Sacraments of Service that equip us to serve others. These four sacraments might be called sacraments for living whole, faithful, and fruitful lives.

REMEMBER

What are the Sacraments of Healing?
Reconciliation and the Anointing of the Sick

What are the three parts of the Sacrament of Penance and Reconciliation?
The three parts of the sacrament are the admission we have done wrong; confession of sins to a priest; and penance—an action that signifies our desire to make things right.

What elements are essential in the marital promises given in Matrimony?
Free consent, a promise of a lifelong, exclusive union, and openness to children

What are the three ordained orders?
Bishops, priests, and deacons

REACH OUT

1. What has been your experience with Reconciliation? Can you do something to make this experience more rewarding?

2. In the past week or so, where has God been present in your life? Write a letter to yourself, reflecting on your relationship with God this week.

Words to Know

confession	penitent
contrition	Penitential Rite
penance	viaticum

REFLECT

The Sacraments of Healing help us realize that God's grace is where we find healing and strength. Write about a time in your life when you most needed God's healing guidance and you asked for it.

_____

_____

_____

_____

_____

_____

_____

_____

Jesus, show me ways to serve others. I especially pray for my family and friends. Protect them and give them what they need. Amen.

Guided by God's
grace

What would a letter of recommendation say about you? What qualities would it highlight? What would it say about how you interact and treat others? Do the words *kind*, *helpful*, *optimistic*, or *dependable* describe your attitude?

One of the scribes . . . asked him, "Which is the first of all the commandments?" Jesus replied, "The first is this: 'Hear, O Israel! The Lord our God is Lord alone! You shall love the Lord your God with all your heart, with all your soul, with all your mind, and with all your strength.' The second is this: 'You shall love your neighbor as yourself.' There is no other commandment greater than these." –Mark 12:28–31

Loving Others

Toward the end of his time on earth, Jesus told a parable about the judgment of human beings at the end of time. Jesus tells the blessed that they are saved because they served him when they fed the hungry, gave drink to the thirsty, welcomed strangers, clothed the naked, cared for the sick, and visited prisoners. In other words, because they loved. (Matthew 25:31–46)

The parable draws attention to the basis of Catholic moral teaching: Every human being should be treated with respect and love because Christ lives in each person. Living a moral life means responding to Jesus' presence in every person, including those who are despised, hungry, thirsty, naked, sick, or imprisoned.

We believe that to love others, no matter who they are, is a way of loving God. Because Christ is present in everyone, there's no fundamental separation between love of God and love of neighbor. If you're looking for a way to experience God, love your neighbor.

A Guide to Living Morally

God gave the Ten Commandments to the Jewish people after he delivered them from slavery in Egypt. He appeared to Moses, the leader of the people, on Mount Sinai in the desert and gave these commands.

The Ten Commandments are the guide to loving God and other people. Another term for them is **the Law of Love.** We usually think of laws as restrictive. But the Law of Love is anything but.

The Law of Love is a law that sets us free. It's like learning how to play tennis. If you don't know the rules, you can't have a game. So you learn the rules. If you don't have the skills to play, you won't enjoy yourself on the court. So you learn how to hold the racket, how to swing, how to position your feet, how to put your body in the right place to return a shot. The rules and skills set you free to play and enjoy the game.

MY TURN: Christ in Others

Think about one key person in your life. How can you see Christ in this person? List the quality of Jesus that you see in him or her.

_____

_____

Describe a time when this person behaved in a way that taught you something about what Jesus was like.

_____

_____

The Ten Commandments

Taken together, the Ten Commandments are a Law of Love that shows us the right way to conduct all our relationships. They describe our responsibilities to God, to our family, to our community, and to society as a whole. They forbid actions that violate the rights of others and bring discord to the world. They direct us to behave with gratitude, honesty, and restraint. No wonder the Jewish people welcomed them as a gift.

Jesus made the Commandments the foundation of his teaching about the moral life. A man asked, "What must I do to inherit eternal life?" Jesus told him to keep the commandments. (Mark 10:17–19) But Jesus had more to say about living rightly. Jesus cared about right actions, but he was especially interested in the condition of our hearts.

Sermon on the Mount, 2010, Laura James.

1. I am the LORD your God: you shall not have strange gods before me.

2. You shall not take the name of the LORD your God in vain.

3. Remember to keep holy the LORD's Day.

4. Honor your father and your mother.

5. You shall not kill.

6. You shall not commit adultery.

7. You shall not steal.

8. You shall not bear false witness against your neighbor.

9. You shall not covet your neighbor's wife.

10. You shall not covet your neighbor's goods.

The Beatitudes

Jesus' teaching about right living is summed up in eight sayings called the Beatitudes, a word that means "blessing." We might call the Beatitudes a program for happiness. They are not about acting the right way, but about becoming the right kind of person. If you are a person of the Beatitudes, you will be happy. You will live with God in Heaven. True happiness lies in mercy, peacemaking, humility, integrity, and dependence on God. Being one of the blessed is not easy, but the reward is great. (Matthew 5:1–10)

Blessed are the poor in spirit,
for theirs is the kingdom of heaven.

Blessed are they who mourn,
for they will be comforted.

Blessed are the meek,
for they will inherit the land.

Blessed are they who hunger and thirst for righteousness,
for they will be satisfied.

Blessed are the merciful,
for they will be shown mercy.

Blessed are the clean of heart,
for they will see God.

Blessed are the peacemakers,
for they will be called children of God.

Blessed are they who are persecuted for the sake of righteousness,
for theirs is the kingdom of heaven.

Virtues

It's important to do the right things, but it's even more important to become the right kind of person, a person with the qualities of the Beatitudes. The Church calls these qualities **virtues.** Virtues are a firm attitude or way of acting that enables us to do good.

Faith, hope, and charity are called the **Theological Virtues** because they are directly related to God and the life of grace we live through the Holy Spirit.

- **Faith** is the ability to believe in God, to obey him, and to commit ourselves personally to him. Part of faith is a trusting relationship with God.

- **Hope** is confidence in God and trust in his promises. It is the power by which we pursue a life of faith.

- **Charity,** or love, is the power by which we give ourselves wholeheartedly to God, to others, and to our part in Christ's mission to save and heal the world. Charity is the greatest virtue.

The **Cardinal Virtues** are prudence, justice, fortitude, and temperance. *Cardinal* comes from the Latin *cardo,* or "hinge." These virtues are the hinges on which the door of the moral life swings.

- **Prudence** is the ability to recognize what is right. It allows us to know what is important, to set the right goals, and to choose the best way to attain them.

- **Justice** is the virtue that longs to see people get what they are entitled to. The just person respects the rights of others and is concerned with fairness. A guiding principle of justice is "to each his due."

MY TURN: Reflection on Sins

Think about the different kinds of sins you witness every day. Write why you think sin is so prevalent.

_____

_____

_____

_____

_____

- **Fortitude,** or courage, is the strength to do what is right in the face of difficulty and opposition. The moral life depends on fortitude because difficulties will inevitably come.

- **Temperance,** or moderation, is the virtue of balance and restraint. A temperate person avoids excess and impulsive judgments. Temperance allows us to balance what we want with what we need.

Sin and Grace

Failure to love God and our neighbor is called sin. We come into the world separated from God—this is called Original Sin, which is washed away at Baptism. But the struggle with sin continues throughout our lives. Happily, we can always count on God to pick us up when we fall. This special help from God is called grace.

Kinds of Sin

Sin comes in many shapes and sizes; one broad distinction has to do with the seriousness of sin. **Venial sins** are less serious offenses; they injure our relationships with God and others. **Mortal sins** are very serious; they reject and grievously harm our relationships with God and others. All sins are to be avoided, but mortal sin is especially grave because it cuts us off from the life of grace. Three conditions must be present to make a sin mortal.

- **Serious matter.** A mortal sin must be a very serious offense. The fact that you think it's serious doesn't necessarily make it a mortal sin.

- **Full knowledge.** You must know how serious the sin is.

- **Full consent.** Knowing that the offense is serious, you freely choose to do it anyway.

Another way we distinguish sins is between **sins of commission** and **sins of omission**. Sins of commission are things you *do;* you lie, you take something that doesn't belong to you; you take revenge on someone who has wronged you. Sins of omission are the things you *don't* do when you have the responsibility to do so. You stand by when a bully abuses someone. You neglect your work. You fail to obey your parents or other authority figures.

SACRED SIGN: Crucifix

The crucifix depicts Jesus Christ on the cross and is a symbol of the Salvation that Jesus gained for us through his Passion and Death. The image of Jesus on a crucifix reminds us of his true human nature. In his human nature, Jesus suffered rejection, humiliation, ridicule, abandonment, and even death on a cross. Born of the Virgin Mary, Jesus was like us in every aspect, except for sin. On the cross and out of love for us, Jesus sacrificed himself for our sins so that we might be saved.

The Seven Capital Sins and Virtues

One helpful classification of sins that Christians have used for centuries is called the seven capital sins. They might be more accurately called "seven deadly attitudes." Sin begins in the heart and mind. These are the negative thoughts and unruly desires that lead to acts that damage a relationship with God and other people. For every sin, there is a redeeming element called a virtue. Virtues lead us to live virtuous, or good, lives.

- **Lust** is an excessive craving for bodily pleasures. You combat lust with the virtue of **chastity.**

- **Greed** is a passionate desire for "more, more, more." A greedy person wants money and possessions for the sake of having them, not because they are needed. Greed is overcome by the virtue of **generosity.**

- **Envy** is to desire to have what someone else has because they have it and you don't. Envy springs from discontent with what you have and is countered by the virtue of **gratitude.**

- **Gluttony** is excessive eating and drinking. The remedy for gluttony is the virtue of **temperance.**

- **Sloth** is laziness and neglect of responsibilities. We can overcome it by practicing the virtue of **zeal.**

- **Anger** is a desire to harm another person in revenge. We overcome anger by cultivating the virtue of **gentleness.**

- **Pride** is self-centeredness, a concern for oneself at the expense of others. The virtue of **humility** is the remedy for pride.

Note that each of the seven deadly attitudes is a distortion of something good: You should feel good about your talents and accomplishments, but this feeling becomes

RITE: Striking the Breast

During the *Confiteor* during Mass in which we pray "through my fault, through my fault, through my most grievous fault," we are asked to strike our breast. This sacramental action is a symbolic tapping of the heart. It signifies regret and sorrow for the sins we have committed, recalling the penitent tax collector in the Gospel of Luke. (18:9–14) Through this gesture and prayer, we recognize our sinfulness while at the same time placing our trust in God's never-ending love.

pride when you decide that it makes you better than other people. It's fine to relax and enjoy yourself. It is sloth when you're so busy relaxing that you ignore your friends, family, schoolwork, and other responsibilities. Most sin comes from a normal human desire taken to excess. Virtues allow us to act within our human condition to be good to others, to ourselves, and to God.

Mercy

Sin is a reality of our lives, but so is God's mercy, and mercy has the last word. **Mercy** is compassion and kindness toward one who is in trouble. It's not something for which we need to beg. God's merciful love delivers us from evil and restores us to grace. When we respond to God's mercy with repentance and contrition, we are restored to the relationship we had with God.

In fact, turning away from sin deepens our relationship with God. Receiving God's mercy allows us to love him more. We can count on God's mercy. It's always there for us.

WITNESS: Saint Monica

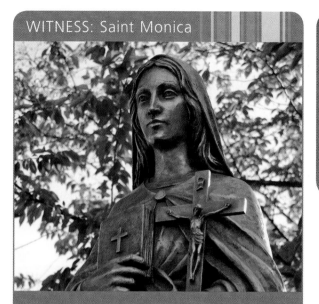

Saint Monica was the mother of Saint Augustine and a good example of one who lived a virtuous life. When he was young, Augustine rejected Christianity, the faith of his mother. Instead he lived a carefree life while searching for answers in different religions. This greatly troubled Monica, who never ceased praying for her son's conversion. She prayed and fasted for her son and stayed close to him, following him from their native North Africa to Rome and Milan. Monica's tears, prayers, and sacrifices over many years helped bring about Augustine's conversion in A.D. 386. Saint Monica's feast day is August 27, the day before the feast day of Saint Augustine.

MY TURN: Showing Mercy

Write of a time when you witnessed someone being merciful toward another. What did you learn from that experience?

_____

_____

_____

_____

summary

FAITH SUMMARY

Catholic moral teaching is based on the principle that all people deserve respect and love because Jesus lives in them. The Ten Commandments, the Beatitudes, and the Church's teaching about virtue give us sure guidance in our responsibilities toward others and in our growth as moral people.

REMEMBER

What are three conditions that must be met to make a sin mortal?

The offense must be a serious one, the person must know it's serious, and the person must freely choose to do it.

Why are the Ten Commandments called the Law of Love?

The Ten Commandments are a gift from our loving God. They show us the way to a life of loving service to God and other people.

How do Jesus' Beatitudes differ from the Ten Commandments?

The Beatitudes are focused on becoming the right kind of person. The Commandments concentrate on right actions.

What are virtues?

Virtues are a firm attitude or way of acting that enables us to do good.

REACH OUT

1. Which of the seven virtues discussed in the chapter would you like to have more of right now? Why?

2. Which of the eight beatitudes is most attractive to you? Which seems the farthest away from your experience? Why?

Words to Know

Cardinal Virtues	the Law of Love
mercy	Theological Virtues
mortal sin	venial sin
sins of commission	virtues
sins of omission	

REFLECT

Think about your personality. Which traits are you most proud of, and which traits would you like to improve?

_____

_____

_____

_____

_____

_____

_____

Father, thank you for your mercy toward me and those I love. When I stumble and sin, help me see my errors and have the strength to not repeat my mistakes. Give me grace to act rightly, and to continue growing in virtue. Amen.

Our Faith in
action

Recall a time when you had to face a big challenge that you weren't sure you could meet. What did you do about it? Did other people help you? How did it turn out? What did you learn about your strengths and your weaknesses?

And the crowds asked him, "What then should we do?" He said to them in reply, "Whoever has two tunics should share with the person who has none. And whoever has food should do likewise."   *–Luke 3:10–11*

We Live in Communities

You are an individual—a person with rights and dignity and a personal relationship with God. You are also part of a community. Actually, you belong to several communities—your family, the Church, your local town or city, your state and nation. You are also a member of the universal human family. A big part of Catholic living is working for the good of others.

Good deeds take our time, energy, and material resources. We do good deeds out of love—because God loves us and calls us to share that love with the people in our lives. Through our good deeds, we grow closer to Christ as we make the world a better place.

Works of Mercy

The traditional Catholic term for good deeds is works of mercy. *Mercy* means "kindness and compassion." Works of mercy put that compassion into practice by bringing blessing and relief to others. **Corporal Works of Mercy** are deeds that meet the material and physical needs of those who are weak and vulnerable. **Spiritual Works of Mercy** are directed to others' spiritual and emotional needs.

Corporal Works of Mercy

The Corporal Works of Mercy are drawn from Jesus' parable about the Last Judgment. In the parable, the blessed are saved because they served Jesus when they fed the hungry, gave drink to the thirsty, sheltered the homeless, clothed the naked, cared for the sick, visited prisoners, and buried the dead. Here are the seven Corporal Works of Mercy, with suggestions about ways to practice them.

MY TURN: Giving and Receiving Mercy

Describe a time when you were in need and received mercy from someone. What were the circumstances? How did someone help you? How did it feel to be helped?

_____

_____

_____

Describe a time when you helped someone in trouble. Was it easy or difficult to do?

_____

_____

_____

_____

comm

Clothing Drive

Feed the Hungry and Give Drink to the Thirsty

Water and food is abundant in our society, yet millions of the world's people don't have enough food to eat or clean water to drink. There are people in your own community who don't have adequate nutrition. You can support food pantries, soup kitchens, other volunteer agencies that feed the hungry with food donations, or donate to organizations that help provide clean, drinkable water to areas without.

Clothe the Naked

Clothing is expensive. Poor families, and many who are not so poor, get much of their clothing from agencies that receive surplus clothing. Go through your drawers and closets, remove clothes that you don't need, and donate them to these agencies. Raise money for your local or diocesan Catholic organization that serves the needy.

Shelter the Homeless

Some people in your own community are literally homeless. You can support agencies that help them. But many others are homeless in a different way. Immigrants and newcomers have trouble feeling at home in your community. There are students in your school who are "different," who lack friends, and who have difficulty fitting in. There are people in your neighborhood, perhaps even in your extended family, who are lonely because they live alone or cannot get around very well. Helping them is a work of mercy.

Visit the Sick

Injury and serious illness remove people from the flow of ordinary life and often cause them to feel lonely, fearful, and depressed. Spend time with sick and elderly family members and neighbors. Organize a class get-well project for a classmate who is ill at home or in the hospital.

Visit the Imprisoned

Prisoners are forgotten by society; people tend to overlook them. You might not have opportunities to visit someone in prison, but you can reach out to those who are "imprisoned" by loneliness, sickness, or old age.

Bury the Dead

In many parts of the world, helping those who are poor see to the proper burial of deceased family members is a work of mercy. In our society we can do this work by being attentive and helpful to those in mourning.

Almsgiving is often thought of as a Corporal Work of Mercy, but it is a work of justice. Jesus led by example when he said, "Whatever you have done to the least of my brethren, you have done to me." (Matthew 25:40) We can be like Jesus when we give alms, or money, to the poor.

unity

Spiritual Works of Mercy

The seven Spiritual Works of Mercy respond to the spiritual and emotional needs of others. The first three often involve a deeper understanding and concentration. The other four can be done by everyone more routinely.

Admonish Sinners

Sometimes it's necessary to warn others about the harm their actions do to themselves and others. To do this effectively, you need to be tactful, knowledgeable, and to have the proper relationship with the person.

Instruct the Ignorant

Look for opportunities to share what you know with others. You can help friends with schoolwork. You can share practical knowledge with younger children.

Counsel the Doubtful

The world is full of cynicism and negativity. Rather than add to it, adopt a positive outlook. It is a work of mercy to share your hope with people who are guarded and depressed.

Comfort the Sorrowful

You may be with people who are discouraged and sad. They may have lost friends or performed poorly in school or sports. They might be troubled by problems at home. It is a work of mercy to comfort them with your friendship.

Bear Wrongs Patiently

When things go wrong for you, do not spread the pain to others. Avoid complaining, criticizing, and blaming. Give others the benefit of the doubt. Overlook minor mistakes and offenses.

Forgive All Injuries

When someone offends or injures you, forgive that person. Holding grudges or trying to get even only worsens the pain. Pray for those who have wronged you. If forgiveness is difficult, pray for the strength to forgive.

Pray for the Living and the Dead

Lift up your needs and those of others in prayer. Pray especially about those problems for which there seem to be no easy solutions.

MY TURN: What to Do?

List some ways you could put some of the Corporal and Spiritual Works of Mercy into practice today.

_____

_____

_____

A Just Society

The love that moves us to do works of mercy is the foundation of Catholic thought. The Church is concerned about politics, economics, and culture because all men and women have dignity and rights that need to be defended and promoted. The Church opposes oppression, exploitation, and other forms of injustice. It upholds freedom, justice, and human well-being for everyone in every society.

The Church's social teaching states that society should be organized to promote political, economic, and social well-being. Catholic Social Teaching states that the rights of people be protected and that principles guide our efforts to work for the good of society as a whole.

Two key principles of Catholic Social Teaching are common good and subsidiarity. **Common good** is the well-being of society as a whole. We work for the common good when we practice the Corporal and Spiritual Works of Mercy, become active in the affairs of our communities, and consider the needs of others when making decisions.

Subsidiarity is the principle that work for the common good ought to be handled by the authority that is closest to the people involved—the most local and least centralized authority. Political decisions should be made at the local level if possible.

Life and Dignity of the Human Person

A just society begins with respect for the dignity of the person. Every human being is created in the image of God and thus has a sacred dignity that no government can erase. Human beings may never be coerced, abused, or exploited in order to achieve a social end. The first responsibility of governments and social institutions is to protect the rights of individuals.

Rights and Responsibilities

A healthy community is one where rights are protected and responsibilities are fulfilled. Every person has a right to life and to the things required for a decent life—starting with food and shelter, employment, health care, and education. Every person also has responsibilities—to one another, to his or her family, and to the common good.

Care for Creation

Human beings are the stewards of God's creation. We have a responsibility to protect and manage creation for the common good.

SACRED SIGN: Religious Habit

The habit is the unique dress or attire wore by men and women who belong to religious orders. Brothers, sisters, friars, nuns, and monks are some of the religious who might wear a habit, although not all of them are required to do so. The habits vary for each religious order, but all of them represent the dedication of the person wearing it to his or her vocation to religious life and to the vows he or she took when he or she became members of the religious order.

Participation in Family and Community

All people have a right to participate in the economic, political, and cultural life of society. No one should be excluded.

Solidarity

Solidarity is the unity of all people in society. The Church urges all people to build just social structures and to work together for the common good. Christians express special solidarity with those who are poor, with whom Jesus identified completely.

Option for the Poor

A basic moral test of a society is how well it treats its most vulnerable members. Those who are poor have a claim on us. Nations as well as individuals are called to take a special concern for the poor and vulnerable because they are most in need of our care and attention. Giving alms to the poor is a work of justice.

Dignity of Work and Workers

People do not serve the economy; the economy must serve people. Workers have basic rights that must be respected. These include the right to productive work, to a fair wage and decent working conditions, to private property, to organize and join unions, and to pursue economic opportunity.

Making Good Choices

The Church lays out a rich program for a virtuous and happy life in the Ten Commandments, the Beatitudes, the works of mercy, and its social teaching. If you follow these moral teachings, you will become the person God created you to be. We do this by making good choices.

You Are Free and Responsible

God created you with **free will**—the ability to make choices of your own accord. God wants you to choose the good, but he does not force you to do the right thing. You need to choose it freely.

Freedom means that you are responsible for everything you do consciously and voluntarily. It is our responsibility to understand the outcomes of our choices and actions and to recognize that some choices lead to bad outcomes.

RITE: The Sign of Peace

The Sign of Peace we exchange at Mass is a sign of hope. It expresses our desire for peace, love, and unity in the Church and among all humanity. Offered before we receive the Eucharist, the Sign of Peace is generally shared as a handshake along with a heartfelt wish that the other person may experience the peace of Christ. By exchanging a Sign of Peace with one another, we are renewing our commitment to be a people who bring about the true peace that only Christ can grant us.

Conscience

The conviction that one choice is right and the other is wrong is called **conscience.** You might think of it as an inner voice telling you what is right. Like freedom, conscience is precious in God's eyes. A person should not be compelled to do anything contrary to his or her conscience.

Right Thinking

Properly forming your conscience begins with humility and being able to see yourself and your actions as they truly are. Consider the effect of your actions on others, and always consider the possibility that your judgment might be wrong. The best safeguard is to learn from experience—ours and that of others.

WITNESS: Saint Francis of Assisi

Saint Francis was born in the town of Assisi, Italy, in 1182. At the age of 20, he devoted himself to a life of prayer. Three years later, Francis embraced a life of poverty and dedicated himself to God. He gave away all his worldly goods and wore only a thin habit as a sign of his dedication to a life of simplicity in solidarity with the poor. Francis was a lover of nature and felt that all plants and animals were part of God's kingdom.

MY TURN: Character-Builders

Your conscience can help shape your character. List one or two traits you possess and explain how you developed those traits within yourself.

_____

_____

_____

_____

_____

summary

FAITH SUMMARY

We put our faith into action by tending to the practical and spiritual needs of others and by working to build a just society. These actions, and other moral choices, require us to learn how to choose well. We must form our consciences properly and think clearly about the moral rightness of our actions.

REMEMBER

What are the Corporal and Spiritual Works of Mercy?

The Corporal Works of Mercy are deeds that meet the material and physical needs of those who are weak and vulnerable. The Spiritual Works of Mercy are directed to others' spiritual and emotional needs.

Why does the Church have social teaching?

The Church is concerned about the right ordering of society because all men and women have rights and dignity that must be defended and promoted.

What is free will?

Free will is our ability to make choices of our own accord. We are free to choose wrong and are responsible for what we do.

What is conscience?

Conscience is the conviction that one choice is right and the other is wrong.

REACH OUT

1. Which of the Corporal Works of Mercy seems easiest for you to do right now? Which seems hardest? Why?

2. What is the most important decision you ever made? How did you go about making it?

Words to Know

common good	solidarity
conscience	Spiritual Works
Corporal Works	of Mercy
of Mercy	subsidiarity
free will	

REFLECT

Write about a time you battled your conscience over what was the right thing to do. Were you happy with your decision?

_____

_____

_____

_____

_____

_____

_____

_____

_____

_____

Jesus, I pray that I may always choose the good. When the way isn't clear, lead me to the help I need. Show me the right way. Amen.

Thanks and
praise

Sometimes things happen in our lives that we wish or need to share with others. During especially difficult times or problems, it is helpful to confide in someone. Recall the last time you just *had* to talk to someone. Whom did you choose to talk to? Why did you choose that person?

"Ask and it will be given to you; seek and you will find; knock and the door will be opened to you. For everyone who asks, receives; and the one who seeks, finds; and to the one who knocks, the door will be opened."
–Matthew 7:7–8

A Connection with God

We usually think about prayer as something *we* do, but it's better to think about it as something *God* does. God made us with a built-in desire to pray. Most people pray. People have always prayed—in every culture and in every time in history. There are prayers for every human need, mood, and temperament. You might say that prayer is as natural to us as breathing. God made us that way.

God reaches out to us. We pray as Christians in response to God's initiative. We pray for something we need because we know that God loves us. We participate in Mass, say traditional prayers, and spend some time thanking Jesus because God has established a relationship with us. We don't have to search for God. God is always there. All we need to do is turn to him.

Types of Prayer

One way to think about prayer is as a communication that goes on between friends. Saint Ignatius of Loyola, one of the greatest spiritual masters, said that we should "talk to God like a friend." God is mighty, holy, and mysterious, but he is also personal and present in our lives. He wants to have a relationship with us, and he has gone to great trouble to establish it.

The five main types of prayer are adoration, petition, intercession, thanksgiving, and praise. Let's look at them through the perspective of communication among friends.

Adoration

Adoration is prayer that recognizes God's greatness and holiness. It recognizes God for who he is. God is great and we are small. But the relationship is still a personal one. Adoration is like spending time with a friend and seeing your friend for who he or she really is.

Petition

Petition is making your needs known to God. God already knows what your needs are. Asking God for what you need is like talking to a friend about your worries, needs, and

MY TURN: Close to My Friends

Describe the time when you felt especially close to someone else—a friend, a brother or sister, an adult. Where were you? What happened between the two of you that made you feel close?

_____

_____

_____

Describe a time when you felt especially close to God. Where were you? What were you thinking and feeling at the time?

_____

_____

problems. Your friend may know quite a bit about what you need, but talking about it builds your friendship and trust.

Intercession

Intercession is prayer for the needs of others. Again, God already knows about them, but talking to him about the needs of your friends, family, and others strengthens your connection with God. It also deepens your sense of being part of a spiritual family in which all care for one another.

Thanksgiving

Gratitude is an important part of every friendship. You thank your friends for the things they do for you. Your deepest gratitude is reserved for God, who has given you everything you have. The greatest prayer of thanksgiving we celebrate is the Eucharistic celebration.

Praise

Prayers of praise express your joy because you know God and love him. You praise God because he exists and because he is good. You do the same thing when you tell your friends how glad you are that they are your friends.

Why We Pray

Prayer for ourselves and others arises naturally in us. When faced with a situation we can't control, we turn to the one who we think can control it. So we pray for rain during a drought, for our team to win the big game, for the healing of a sick person, for help passing an exam, for peace in the world. But God already knows about the

drought and the game and the exam. We don't really think he is weighing his options, deciding which team will win or whether you will pass or fail, based on the quality of prayers. So why pray for these things at all?

We are praying to align our will with God's will. We are telling God that we care deeply about the drought and our relative's illness and the other problems, and that we want to see God at work no matter how these situations turn out. It's easy to see God at work when the situations turn out the way we wish. But he's also there when they don't. Our deepest desire is to see a gravely ill relative recover, but if she doesn't, we want God to comfort us and help us see that death is not the end. We want the drought to end, but if it goes on, we want God to be with us in a challenging time. We want to pass the exam, but, at a deeper level, we want a clear head and steady nerves so we can do our best.

Our prayers mean that we are confident that we are not alone—that God is with us.

Ways to Pray

Christians pray in three ways—with our lips (vocal prayer), in our mind (meditation) and in our heart (contemplation).

Vocal Prayer

Using words, or **vocal prayer,** is the most natural form of prayer. This is where prayer begins for most people. The words can be spoken aloud or prayed in the silence of your heart. They can be your own words or the words of traditional prayers like the Lord's Prayer and the Hail Mary. You can pray by yourself or with others at Mass or other worship services.

connection

The Church passes **traditional prayers** down through the centuries like precious family heirlooms. They enable groups of people to pray in unison. The words of many traditional prayers like the Psalms are beautiful and capable of moving the heart profoundly.

Spontaneous prayers can feel more personal because we use our own words to reflect on our relationship with God. There are many ways to pray spontaneously, such as giving thanks for all the blessings of our lives, identifying our needs and telling God what's on our minds, asking for forgiveness and forgiving others who have done us wrong, thinking about the needs of others, or giving yourself some quiet time with God and listening for anything God has to say to you.

Meditation

Meditation is reflective prayer that seeks awareness of God's presence and understanding of God's work in our lives. It is usually aided by a passage from Scripture, a text from a spiritual writer, or a sacred image. More than other forms of prayer, meditation engages the mind and the imagination. The Rosary combines vocal prayer and meditation. We meditate on events in the lives of Jesus and Mary as we pray the words of the Lord's Prayer, the Hail Mary, and the Glory Be to the Father.

Imaginative prayer uses the Gospels and Scripture readings to help us focus our prayer. We can read a passage from the Gospels and imagine ourselves as a participant in the scene, speaking to and witnessing Jesus. Using our imaginations this way makes Jesus powerfully present to us.

MY TURN: Ask for What You Need

Imagine that you are with Jesus in his ministry. He asks you what you need. What do you say?

_____

_____

_____

Jesus asks you what other people you know need. What do you tell him?

_____

_____

_____

A review of your day is also an excellent form of meditation. It helps you look for the ways that God has been active in your life. Saint Ignatius of Loyola developed a review called the **daily examen** in order to help him see God's hand at work in his daily experiences. A framework based on Saint Ignatius's daily examen is as follows:

- Pray for light. Begin by asking God for the grace to pray, to see, and to understand.

- Give thanks. Look at your day in a spirit of gratitude. Recognize that everything is a gift from God.

- Review the day. Guided by the Holy Spirit, look back on your day. Pay attention to your experiences. Look for God in them throughout your day.

- Look at what's wrong. Face up to failures and shortcomings. Ask forgiveness for your faults. Ask God to show you ways to improve.

- Make resolutions for the day to come. Think of what is currently happening in your life and ask God for guidance, strength, patience, or support. Think of where you may need God specifically.

Contemplation

Contemplative prayer is simply resting quietly in God's presence. It is prayer without words and without ideas. Meditation involves actively focusing on God with the mind and imagination. **Contemplation** is prayer of the heart. It is simply enjoying God.

Centering prayer is a popular form of contemplation that seeks to open our hearts to receive God's gift of grace. It centers on a sacred word or a brief phrase to help us empty our minds and make us receptive to God. A centering prayer does not have to follow a certain order, but it may help to focus on a sacred word or phrase that means something, for example, "Jesus," "Peace," "Grace," "Come Holy Spirit." Using a sacred word to express our desire to be receptive to God's grace can help us refocus our attention if our minds stray.

Regular Prayer

There are no set rules for prayer; it's best to find the style of prayer that suits you best. Forming a regular habit of prayer will be rewarding and enriching. Here are some ideas to get started:

- Set aside time to pray regularly. Make it a habit. This makes prayer part of your life, not something extra added on.

- Keep going with prayer even when it is hard. You will have dry times in prayer, just as you have dry times in any relationship.

- Keep it simple. Be direct and personal. Talk to Jesus as a friend and brother. God is near.

SACRED SIGN: The Paschal Candle

At Baptism, we receive a candle that symbolizes the light of Christ and the flame of faith. The flame used to light this candle is always taken from the Easter candle, also known as the Paschal Candle. The Paschal Candle is blessed and lit from a new fire at the Easter Vigil on Holy Saturday when we celebrate the Death and Resurrection of Jesus. The Paschal Candle is usually decorated with a cross, five grains of incense to symbolize the wounds of Christ, the numerals of the current calendar year, and the Greek letters alpha and omega to signify Christ as "the beginning and the end." It is lit as a Resurrection symbol for Baptisms and funerals.

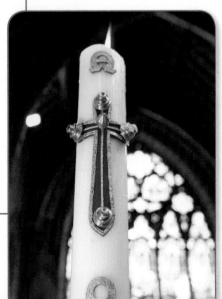

Lord, Teach Us to Pray

The model for direct, simple, personal prayer is the Lord's Prayer. Jesus himself gave it to the disciples when they asked him: "Lord, teach us to pray . . ." (Luke 11:1)

This short but powerful Christian prayer addresses seven petitions to God. The first three have to do with God. The other four have to do with our needs.

Our Father, who art in heaven,

Father means that we are close to God. The relationship is a personal one. It is "our" Father, not "my" Father. We are all brothers and sisters, in one family.

These are words of praise. Heaven is the glorious presence of God. We come into this presence as we pray.

hallowed be thy name;

This is the first of the seven petitions. *Hallowed* means "holy," so this line is saying that God is holy. It is also a prayer that all people will see the holiness of God.

thy kingdom come,

An earthly kingdom is defined by geographical boundaries. God's kingdom is located in the hearts and minds of human beings.

thy will be done
on earth as it is in heaven.

Happiness comes when our wills are aligned with God's. We pray for ourselves and that all nations will embrace the love that God wills for all humankind.

Give us this day our daily bread,

This prayer means that we must consider our own responsibility for those in the world who lack the basic necessities of life.

RITE: Kneeling

Kneeling is a ritual gesture we use to express homage, reverence, petition, and worship. We kneel in the liturgical celebrations of the Church, especially at Mass, during the consecration and before receiving Holy Communion; when we genuflect; and when we adore the Blessed Sacrament. Kneeling, together with our words, songs, symbols and moments of silence helps us express more fully our loving relationship with God.

and forgive us our trespasses, as we forgive those who trespass against us;

We pray to be forgiven for our sins and for help forgiving others. This prayer recognizes that mercy cannot penetrate our hearts if they are hardened with grudges and resentments.

and lead us not into temptation,

We ask the Father to give us the help we need to stay out of trouble. We do not grow in virtue and stay free of sin through our own wisdom and strength. This happens because God has answered this prayer.

but deliver us from evil.

Evil afflicts the world in many ways—war, injustice, poverty, greed, and cruelty of many kinds. We bring all these miseries to our Father and beg him to free us from them.

Pray Without Ceasing

The heart of prayer is the awareness of God's presence in our life. Since God is always there, it is possible to pray at any time. In fact, the real goal of prayer is to be constantly aware that God is our Father, Jesus is our brother, and the Holy Spirit is with us. Prayer is everything we do to recognize God and respond to him.

WITNESS: Saint Thérèse of Lisieux

Saint Thérèse of Lisieux (1873–1897) was a French Carmelite nun whose winning personality and popular writings about prayer made her one of the most popular saints of the 20th century. She called her approach to God "The Little Way." She did not aspire to great deeds but sought sanctity in faithfulness to little things: "every little sacrifice, every glance and word, and the doing of the least actions for love." In the convent, Thérèse dedicated her life to praying for others, especially the missionaries. Recognizing her impact on Catholic spirituality, Thérèse was declared a Doctor of the Church in 1997. She is one of only three female Doctors of the Church.

MY TURN: Prayer for Others

Think of a news story that you heard recently. Write a brief prayer to God on behalf of the people involved, whether they are going through a difficult time or are experiencing good fortune.

_____

_____

_____

summary

FAITH SUMMARY

Prayer is lifting our minds and hearts to God. In prayer we recognize God's holiness, bring our needs and the needs of others to him, thank him for the blessings we have received, and praise him for his goodness. In prayer we become aware of God's continual, active presence in our lives.

REMEMBER

What are the five main types of prayer?

The five main types of prayer are adoration, petition, intercession, thanksgiving, and praise.

Why pray for what we need when God already knows everything about us?

We bring our needs to God as we would to one of our friends on earth. Prayers of petition and intercession strengthen our relationship with God.

What are three ways to pray?

We pray in three ways—with the lips (vocal prayer), in the mind (meditation), and in the heart (contemplation).

What does it mean to pray always?

The real goal of prayer is to be aware of God's constant presence. We can pray always by recognizing God in all things.

REACH OUT

1. Which of the methods of prayer described here would you most like to try? Why?

2. What is the best experience you ever had in prayer? Describe it.

Words to Know

adoration	meditation
centering prayer	petition
contemplation	spontaneous
daily examen	prayers
imaginative prayer	traditional prayers
intercession	vocal prayer

REFLECT

Think about your life at this moment. Reflect on what you learned about the foundations of our faith. Write a daily examen telling God how you hope to live what you have learned. Remember that this is private and you will not be asked to share your responses.

_____

_____

_____

_____

_____

_____

_____

_____

_____

Lord Jesus, I look to you for strength and guidance. Teach me to pray as you taught the disciples. I offer you my prayer of thanks. Amen.

Catholic beliefs and practices

Living Our Faith

As believers in Jesus Christ, we are called to a new life and to make moral choices that keep us united with God. With the help and grace of the Holy Spirit, we can choose ways to act to remain friends with God, to help other people, and to fulfill our prophetic mission to be witnesses to Christ in all circumstances and at the very heart of the human community.

The Ten Commandments

The Ten Commandments are a special expression of natural law made known to us by God's Revelation and by human reason. They guide us in making choices that allow us to live as God wants us to live. The first three commandments tell us how to love God; the rest show us how to love our neighbor.

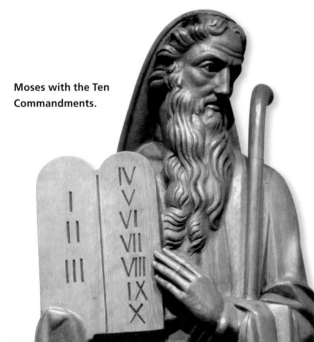

Moses with the Ten Commandments.

1. I am the Lord your God: you shall not have strange gods before me.

2. You shall not take the name of the Lord your God in vain.

3. Remember to keep holy the Lord's Day.

4. Honor your father and your mother.

5. You shall not kill.

6. You shall not commit adultery.

7. You shall not steal.

8. You shall not bear false witness against your neighbor.

9. You shall not covet your neighbor's wife.

10. You shall not covet your neighbor's goods.

The Great Commandment

The Ten Commandments are fulfilled in Jesus' Great Commandment: "You shall love the LORD your God with all your heart, with all your soul, with all your mind, and with all your strength. . . . You shall love your neighbor as yourself." (Mark 12:30–31)

The New Commandment

Before his death on the cross, Jesus gave his disciples a new commandment: "[L]ove one another. As I have loved you, so you also should love one another." (John 13:34)

Sermon on the Mount, **15th Century.**

The Beatitudes

The Beatitudes are the teachings of Jesus in the Sermon on the Mount. (Matthew 5:3–10)

Jesus teaches us that if we live according to the Beatitudes, we will live a happy Christian life. The Beatitudes fulfill God's promises made to Abraham and his descendants and describe the rewards that will be ours as loyal followers of Christ.

Blessed are the poor in spirit,
  for theirs is the kingdom of heaven.

Blessed are they who mourn,
  for they will be comforted.

Blessed are the meek,
  for they will inherit the land.

Blessed are they who hunger and thirst
  for righteousness,
    for they will be satisfied.

Blessed are the merciful,
  for they will be shown mercy.

Blessed are the clean of heart,
  for they will see God.

Blessed are the peacemakers,
  for they will be called children of God.

Blessed are they who are persecuted
  for the sake of righteousness,
    for theirs is the kingdom of heaven.

Works of Mercy

The Corporal and Spiritual Works of Mercy are actions that extend God's compassion and mercy to those in need.

Corporal Works of Mercy

The Corporal Works of Mercy are kind acts by which we help our neighbors with their material and physical needs. They include

feed the hungry

give drink to the thirsty

clothe the naked

shelter the homeless

visit the sick

visit the imprisoned

bury the dead

Spiritual Works of Mercy

The Spiritual Works of Mercy are acts of compassion that serve people's emotional and spiritual needs. They include

Counsel the doubtful	**Instruct the ignorant**
Admonish sinners	**Comfort the afflicted**
Forgive offenses	**Bear wrongs patiently**
Pray for the living and the dead	

Precepts of the Church

The Precepts of the Church describe the minimum effort we must make in prayer and in living a moral life. All Catholics are called to move beyond the minimum by growing in love of God and love of neighbor. The Precepts are as follows:

1. attendance at Mass on Sundays and Holy Days of Obligation

2. confession of sins at least once a year

3. reception of Holy Communion at least once a year during the Easter season

4. observance of the days of fast and abstinence

5. providing for the needs of the Church

Days of Fast
(for Adults)

Ash Wednesday   Good Friday

Days of Abstinence
(for all those over 14)

Ash Wednesday   All Fridays in Lent

Holy Days of Obligation

Holy Days of Obligation are the days other than Sundays on which we celebrate the great things God has done for us through Jesus and the saints. On Holy Days of Obligation, Catholics are obliged to attend Mass. Six Holy Days of Obligation are celebrated in the United States.

Mary, Mother of God
January 1

Ascension
Forty days after Easter (for those dioceses that do not celebrate the Ascension on the seventh Sunday of Easter)

Assumption of the Blessed Virgin Mary
August 15

All Saints
November 1

Immaculate Conception
December 8

Nativity of Our Lord Jesus Christ
December 25

Ascension of Jesus.

We celebrate Mary's life on several Holy Days of Obligation.

83

Virtues

Virtues are gifts from God that lead us to live in a close relationship with him. Virtues are like good habits. They need to be used; they can be lost if they are neglected. The three most important virtues are called the Theological Virtues because they come from God and lead to God. The Cardinal Virtues are human virtues, acquired by education and good actions. They are named for the Latin word for "hinge" (*cardo*), meaning "that on which other things depend."

Theological Virtues

faith   **charity**   **hope**

Cardinal Virtues

prudence   **justice**

fortitude   **temperance**

Gifts of the Holy Spirit

The Holy Spirit makes it possible for us to do what God the Father asks of us by giving us many gifts. They include the following:

wisdom   **counsel**

knowledge   **understanding**

fortitude   **fear of the Lord**

piety

Fruits of the Holy Spirit

The Fruits of the Holy Spirit are examples of the way we find ourselves acting because God is alive in us. They include the following:

love   **joy**   **peace**

kindness   **generosity**   **goodness**

gentleness   **self-control**   **modesty**

faithfulness   **chastity**   **patience**

Left to right: the Theogical Virtues of charity, faith, and hope, Heinrich Maria von Hess, 1819.

Making Good Choices

Our conscience is the inner voice that helps us know the law God has placed in our hearts. Our conscience helps us judge the moral qualities of our own actions. It guides us to do good and avoid evil.

The Holy Spirit can help us form a good conscience. We form our conscience by studying the teachings of the Church and following the guidance of our parents and pastoral leaders.

God has given every human being freedom of choice. This does not mean that we have the right to do whatever we please. We can live in true freedom if we cooperate with the Holy Spirit, who gives us the virtue of prudence. This virtue helps us recognize what is good in every situation and make correct choices. The Holy Spirit gives us the gifts of wisdom and understanding to help us make the right choices in life, in relationship to God and others. The gift of counsel helps us reflect on making the correct choices in life.

Showing Our Love for the World

In the story of the Good Samaritan (Luke 10:29–37), Jesus makes clear our responsibility to care for those in need. The Catholic Church teaches this responsibility in the following themes of Catholic Social Teaching.

Life and Dignity of the Human Person

All human life is sacred, and all people must be respected and valued over material goods. We are called to ask whether our actions as a society respect or threaten the life and dignity of the human person.

Call to Family, Community, and Participation

Participation in family and community is central to our faith and a healthy society. Families must be supported so that people can participate in society, build a community spirit, and promote the well-being of all, especially those who are poor and vulnerable.

Rights and Responsibilities

Every person has a right to life as well as a right to those things required for human decency. As Catholics, we have a responsibility to protect these basic human rights in order to achieve a healthy society.

Option for the Poor and Vulnerable

In our world, many people are very rich while at the same time many are extremely poor. As Catholics, we are called to pay special attention to the needs of the poor by defending and promoting their dignity and meeting their immediate material needs.

The Dignity of Work and the Rights of Workers

The Catholic Church teaches that the basic rights of workers must be respected: the right to productive work, fair wages, and private property; and the right to organize, join unions, and pursue economic opportunity. Catholics believe that the economy is meant to serve people and that work is not merely a way to make a living, but an important way in which we participate in God's creation.

Solidarity

Because God is our Father, we are all brothers and sisters with the responsibility to care for one another. Solidarity is the attitude that leads Christians to share spiritual and material goods. Solidarity unites rich and poor, weak and strong, and helps create a society that recognizes that we all depend on one another.

Care for God's Creation

God is the Creator of all people and all things, and he wants us to enjoy his creation. The responsibility to care for all God has made is a requirement of our faith.

Celebrating Our Faith

Jesus touches our lives through the sacraments. In the sacraments, physical objects—water, bread and wine, oil, and others—are the signs of Jesus' presence.

The Seven Sacraments

Sacraments of Initiation

These sacraments lay the foundation of every Christian life.

Baptism

In Baptism we are born into new life in Christ. Baptism takes away Original Sin and makes us members of the Church. One of its signs is the pouring of water.

Confirmation

Confirmation seals our life of faith in Jesus. Its signs are the laying on of hands on a person's head, most often by a bishop, and the anointing with oil. Like Baptism, it is received only once.

Eucharist

The Eucharist nourishes our life of faith. We receive the Body and Blood of Christ under the appearance of bread and wine.

Sacraments of Healing

These sacraments celebrate the healing power of Jesus.

Penance and Reconciliation

Through Reconciliation we receive God's forgiveness. Forgiveness requires being sorry for our sins. In Reconciliation we receive Jesus' healing grace through absolution by the priest. The signs of this sacrament are our confession of sins, our repentance and satisfaction, and the words of absolution.

Anointing of the Sick

This sacrament unites a sick person's sufferings with those of Jesus. Oil, a symbol of strength, is a sign of this sacrament. A person is anointed with oil and receives the laying on of hands from a priest.

Sacraments at the Service of Communion

These sacraments help us serve the community.

Matrimony

In Matrimony a baptized man and woman are united with each other as a sign of the unity between Jesus and his Church. Matrimony requires the consent of the couple, as expressed in the marriage promises. The couple are the sign of this sacrament.

Holy Orders

In Holy Orders, men are ordained priests to be leaders of the community, or deacons to be reminders of our baptismal call to serve others. The signs of this sacrament are the laying on of hands and the prayer of the bishop asking God for the outpouring of the Holy Spirit by the bishop.

Reconciling with God and Others

An Examination of Conscience

An examination of conscience is the act of prayerfully looking into our hearts to ask how we have hurt our relationships with God and other people through our thoughts, words, and actions. We reflect on the Ten Commandments and the teachings of the Church. The questions below will help us in our examination of conscience.

My Relationship with God

- What steps am I taking to help myself grow closer to God and others? Do I turn to God often during the day, especially when I am tempted?

- Do I participate at Mass with attention and devotion on Sundays and Holy Days? Do I pray often and read the Bible?

- Do I use God's name or the name of Jesus, Mary, and the saints with love and reverence?

My Relationship with Family, Friends, and Neighbors

- Have I set a bad example through my words or actions? Do I treat others fairly? Do I spread stories that hurt other people?

- Am I loving of those in my family? Am I respectful to my neighbors, friends, and those in authority?

- Do I show respect for my body and for the bodies of others? Do I keep away from forms of entertainment that do not respect God's gift of sexuality?

- Have I taken or damaged anything that did not belong to me? Have I cheated, copied homework, or lied?

- Do I quarrel with others just so I can get my own way? Do I insult others to try to make them think they are less than I am? Do I hold grudges and try to hurt people who I think have hurt me?

How to Make a Good Confession

An examination of conscience is an important part of preparing for the Sacrament of Reconciliation. The Sacrament of Reconciliation includes the following steps:

1. The priest greets us and we pray the Sign of the Cross. He may read God's Word with us.

2. We confess our sins. The priest may help and counsel us.

3. The priest gives us a penance to perform. Our penance may be prayers to be prayed, an act of kindness, or both.

4. The priest asks us to express our sorrow, usually by reciting the Act of Contrition.

5. We receive absolution. The priest says, "I absolve you from your sins in the name of the Father, and of the Son, and of the Holy Spirit." We respond, "Amen."

6. The priest dismisses us by saying, "Go in peace." We go forth to perform the act of penance he has given us.

The Eucharist

Sunday is the day on which we celebrate the Resurrection of Jesus. Sunday is the Lord's Day. We gather for Mass, rest from work, and perform Works of Mercy. People from all over the world gather at God's Eucharistic table as brothers and sisters on the Lord's Day.

The Order of Mass

The Mass is the high point of the Christian life, and it always follows a set order.

Introductory Rites

We prepare to celebrate the Eucharist.

Entrance Chant

We gather as a community praising God in song.

Greeting

We pray the Sign of the Cross, recognizing the presence of Christ in the community.

Penitential Act

We acknowledge our sins and ask God for mercy.

Gloria

We praise God in song.

Collect Prayer

The priest gathers all our prayers into one.

Liturgy of the Word

We hear the story of God's plan for Salvation.

First Reading

We listen to God's Word, usually from the Old Testament.

Responsorial Psalm

We respond to God's Word, usually in song.

Second Reading

We listen to God's Word from the New Testament.

Gospel Acclamation

We sing or pray "Alleluia!" to praise God for the Good News. During Lent a different acclamation is used.

Gospel Reading

We stand to acclaim Christ present in the Gospel.

Homily

The priest or deacon explains God's Word.

Profession of Faith

We proclaim our faith through the Creed.

Prayer of the Faithful

We pray for our needs and the needs of others.

Liturgy of the Eucharist

We celebrate the meal that Jesus instituted at the Last Supper and remember the sacrifice he made for us.

Presentation and Preparation of the Gifts

We bring gifts of bread and wine to the altar.

Prayer over the Offerings

The priest prays that God will accept our sacrifice.

Eucharistic Prayer

This prayer of thanksgiving is the center and high point of the entire celebration.

Preface Dialogue

We give thanks and praise to God.

Preface Acclamation
(or Holy, Holy, Holy)

We sing an acclamation of praise.

Institution Narrative

The bread and wine truly become the Body and Blood of Jesus Christ.

The Mystery of Faith

We proclaim Jesus' Death and Resurrection.

Communion Rite

We prepare to receive the Body and Blood of Jesus Christ.

The Lord's Prayer

We pray the Lord's Prayer.

Sign of Peace

We offer one another Christ's peace.

Lamb of God

We pray for forgiveness, mercy, and peace.

Communion

We receive the Body and Blood of Jesus Christ.

Prayer after Communion

We pray that the Eucharist will strengthen us to live as Jesus Christ did.

Laura James, *Amen,* 2010.

Concluding Rites

At the conclusion of Mass, we are blessed and sent forth.

Final Blessing

We receive God's blessing.

Dismissal

We go in peace to glorify the Lord in our lives.

Devotions of Our Faith

Prayers to Take to Heart

We can pray with any words that come to mind. Sometimes, when we find that choosing our own words is difficult, we can use traditional prayers. Likewise, when we pray aloud with others, we rely on traditional prayers to unite our minds, hearts, and voices. Memorizing traditional prayers such as the following can be very helpful. When we memorize prayers, we take them to heart, meaning that we not only learn the words but also try to understand and live them.

Sign of the Cross

In the name of the Father
and of the Son
and of the Holy Spirit.
Amen.

Lord's Prayer

Our Father, who art in heaven,
hallowed be thy name;
thy kingdom come,
thy will be done
on earth as it is in heaven.
Give us this day our daily bread,
and forgive us our trespasses,
as we forgive those who trespass against us;
and lead us not into temptation,
but deliver us from evil.
Amen.

Glory Be to the Father

Glory be to the Father
and to the Son
and to the Holy Spirit,
as it was in the beginning
is now, and ever shall be
world without end.
Amen.

Hail Mary

Hail, Mary, full of grace,
the Lord is with thee.
Blessed art thou among women,
and blessed is the fruit of thy womb, Jesus.
Holy Mary, Mother of God,
pray for us sinners,
now and at the hour of our death.
Amen.

Morning Prayer

God, our Father, I offer you today all that I think
    and do and say.
I offer it with what was done on earth
by Jesus Christ, your Son.
Amen.

Grace Before Meals

Bless us, O Lord, and these thy gifts,
which we are about to receive from thy bounty,
through Christ our Lord.
Amen.

Grace After Meals

We give thee thanks for all thy benefits,
Almighty God, who live and reign for ever.
And may the souls of the faithful departed,
through the mercy of God, rest in peace.
Amen.

prayers

Nicene Creed

I believe in one God,
the Father almighty,
maker of heaven and earth,
of all things visible and invisible.

I believe in one Lord Jesus Christ,
the Only Begotten Son of God,
born of the Father before all ages.
God from God, Light from Light,
true God from true God,
begotten, not made, consubstantial with
    the Father;
through him all things were made.
For us men and for our salvation
he came down from heaven,
and by the Holy Spirit was incarnate of the
    Virgin Mary,
and became man.

For our sake he was crucified under
    Pontius Pilate,
he suffered death and was buried,
and rose again on the third day
in accordance with the Scriptures.
He ascended into heaven
and is seated at the right hand of the Father.
He will come again in glory
to judge the living and the dead
and his kingdom will have no end.

I believe in the Holy Spirit, the Lord,
    the giver of life,
who proceeds from the Father and the Son,
who with the Father and the Son is adored
    and glorified,
who has spoken through the prophets.

I believe in one, holy, catholic and
    apostolic Church.
I confess one Baptism for the forgiveness of sins
and I look forward to the resurrection
    of the dead
and the life of the world to come.
Amen.

The Apostles' Creed

I believe in God,
the Father almighty,
Creator of heaven and earth,
and in Jesus Christ, his only Son, our Lord,
who was conceived by the Holy Spirit,
born of the Virgin Mary,
suffered under Pontius Pilate,
was crucified, died and was buried;
he descended into hell;
on the third day he rose again from the dead;
he ascended into heaven,
and is seated at the right hand of God the
    Father almighty;
from there he will come to judge the living
    and the dead.

I believe in the Holy Spirit,
the holy catholic Church,
the communion of saints,
the forgiveness of sins,
the resurrection of the body,
and life everlasting.
Amen.

Act of Contrition
(or Prayer of the Penitent)

My God,
I am sorry for my sins with all my heart.
In choosing to do wrong
and failing to do good,
I have sinned against you
whom I should love above all things.
I firmly intend, with your help,
to do penance,
to sin no more,
and to avoid whatever leads me to sin.
Our Savior Jesus Christ
suffered and died for us.
In his name, my God, have mercy.
Amen.

Act of Faith

O my God, I firmly believe
that you are one God in three divine Persons,
Father, Son, and Holy Spirit.
I believe that your divine Son became man
and died for our sins, and that he will come
to judge the living and the dead.
I believe these and all the truths
which the Holy Catholic Church teaches,
because you have revealed them
who are eternal truth and wisdom,
who can neither deceive nor be deceived.
In this faith I intend to live and die.
Amen.

Act of Hope

O Lord God,
I hope by your grace for the pardon
of all my sins
and after life here to gain
   eternal happiness
because you have promised it
who are infinitely powerful,
   faithful, kind,
      and merciful.
In this hope I intend to live and die.
Amen.

Act of Love

O Lord God, I love you above all things
and I love my neighbor for your sake
because you are the highest, infinite
   and perfect good, worthy of all my love.
In this love I intend to live and die.
Amen.

Prayer to the Holy Spirit

Come, Holy Spirit, fill the hearts of
   your faithful.
And kindle in them the fire of your love.
Send forth your Spirit and they shall
   be created.
And you shall renew the face of the earth.

Let us pray:
O God, by the light of the Holy Spirit you have
taught the hearts of your faithful. In the same
Spirit, help us to know what is truly right and
always rejoice in your consolation. We ask this
through Christ, Our Lord.
Amen.

Angelus

V. The Angel of the Lord declared unto Mary.
R. And she conceived of the Holy Spirit.
Hail, Mary, full of grace, . . .

V. Behold the handmaid of the Lord.
R. Be it done unto me according to thy word.
      Hail Mary.

V. And the Word was made flesh.
R. And dwelt among us.
      Hail Mary.

V. Pray for us, O holy Mother of God,
R. That we may be made worthy of the
      promises of Christ.

Let us pray;
Pour forth, we beseech thee, O Lord, thy
grace into our hearts; that we, to whom
the Incarnation of Christ, thy Son, was made
known by the message of an angel, may by
his Passion and Cross be brought to the glory
of his Resurrection. Through the same Christ
our Lord.
Amen.

Memorare

Remember, O most gracious Virgin Mary,
that never was it known
that anyone who fled to thy protection,
implored thy help,
or sought thy intercession,
was left unaided.
Inspired by this confidence
I fly unto thee,
O Virgin of virgins, my Mother.
To thee do I come,
before thee I stand,
sinful and sorrowful.
O Mother of the Word Incarnate,
despise not my petitions,
but in thy mercy hear and answer me.
Amen.

Magnificat

My soul proclaims the greatness of the Lord,
my spirit rejoices in God my Savior,
for he has looked with favor on his lowly servant.
From this day all generations will call me blessed:
the Almighty has done great things for me,
and holy is his Name.
He has mercy on those who fear him
  in every generation.
He has shown the strength of his arm,
he has scattered the proud in their conceit.
He has cast down the mighty from their thrones,
and has lifted up the lowly.
He has filled the hungry with good things,
and the rich he has sent away empty.
He has come to the help of his servant Israel
for he has remembered his promise of mercy,
the promise he made to our fathers,
to Abraham and his children forever.

Queen of Heaven (Regina Caeli)

Queen of heaven, rejoice. alleluia.
The Son whom you merited to bear, alleluia,
has risen as he said, alleluia.
Rejoice and be glad, O Virgin Mary, alleluia.
For the Lord has truly risen, alleluia.

Let us pray;
O God, who through the resurrection of your
Son, our Lord Jesus Christ, did vouchsafe to
give joy to the world; grant, we beseech you,
that through his Mother, the virgin Mary, we
may obtain the joys of everlasting life.
Through the same Christ our Lord.
Amen.

Hail Holy Queen (Salve Regina)

Hail, Holy Queen, Mother of Mercy,
our life, our sweetness and our hope.
To you do we cry,
poor banished children of Eve.
To you do we send up our sighs,
mourning and weeping in this valley of tears.
Turn then, most gracious advocate,
your eyes of mercy toward us,
and after this exile
show unto us the blessed fruit of thy womb,
  Jesus.
O clement, O loving,
O sweet Virgin Mary.

Praying the Rosary

The Rosary helps us pray to Jesus through Mary. When we pray the Rosary, we think about the special events, or mysteries, in the lives of Jesus and Mary.

The Rosary is made up of a string of beads and a crucifix. We hold the crucifix in our hand as we pray the Sign of the Cross. Then we pray the Apostles' Creed.

Following the crucifix there is a single bead, followed by a set of three beads and another single bead. We pray the Lord's Prayer as we hold the first single bead, and a Hail Mary at each bead in the set of three that follows. Then we pray the Glory Be to the Father. On the next single bead, we think about the first mystery and pray the Lord's Prayer.

There are 5 sets of 10 beads; each set is called a decade. We pray a Hail Mary on each bead of a decade as we reflect on a particular mystery in the lives of Jesus and Mary. The Glory Be to the Father is prayed at the end of each decade. Between decades is a single bead on which we think about one of the

mysteries and pray the Lord's Prayer. We end by holding the crucifix in our hands as we pray the Sign of the Cross.

9. Pray ten Hail Marys and one Glory Be to the Father.

10. Think about the fourth mystery. Pray the Lord's Prayer.

8. Think about the third mystery. Pray the Lord's Prayer.

11. Pray ten Hail Marys and one Glory Be to the Father.

7. Pray ten Hail Marys and one Glory Be to the Father.

6. Think about the second mystery. Pray the Lord's Prayer.

12. Think about the fifth mystery. Pray the Lord's Prayer.

5. Pray ten Hail Marys and one Glory Be to the Father.

13. Pray ten Hail Marys and one Glory Be to the Father.

4. Think about the first mystery. Pray the Lord's Prayer.

Pray the Hail, Holy Queen. Many people pray the Hail, Holy Queen after the last decade.

3. Pray three Hail Marys and one Glory Be to the Father.

2. Pray the Lord's Prayer.

14. Pray the Sign of the Cross.

1. Pray the Sign of the Cross and the Apostles' Creed.

The Mysteries of the Rosary

The Church has used three sets of mysteries for many years. In 2002 Pope John Paul II proposed a fourth set of mysteries, the Mysteries of Light, or the Luminous Mysteries. According to his suggestion, the mysteries might be prayed on the following days: the Joyful Mysteries on Monday and Saturday, the Sorrowful Mysteries on Tuesday and Friday, the Glorious Mysteries on Wednesday and Sunday, and the Luminous Mysteries on Thursday.

The Joyful Mysteries

1. **The Annunciation**
   Mary learns that she has been chosen to be the mother of Jesus.

2. **The Visitation**
   Mary visits Elizabeth, who tells Mary that she will always be remembered.

3. **The Nativity**
   Jesus is born in a stable in Bethlehem.

4. **The Presentation**
   Mary and Joseph bring the infant Jesus to the Temple to present him to God.

5. **The Finding of Jesus in the Temple**
   Jesus is found in the Temple discussing his faith with the teachers.

The Luminous Mysteries

1. **The Baptism of Jesus in the River Jordan**
   God the Father proclaims that Jesus is his beloved Son.

2. **The Wedding Feast at Cana**
   At Mary's request, Jesus performs his first miracle.

3. **The Proclamation of the Kingdom of God**
   Jesus calls all to conversion and service to the kingdom.

4. **The Transfiguration of Jesus**
   Jesus is revealed in glory to Peter, James, and John.

5. **The Institution of the Eucharist**
   Jesus offers his Body and Blood at the Last Supper.

The Sorrowful Mysteries

1. **The Agony in the Garden**
   Jesus prays in the Garden of Gethsemane on the night before he dies.

2. **The Scourging at the Pillar**
   Jesus is lashed with whips.

3. **The Crowning with Thorns**
   Jesus is mocked and crowned with thorns.

4. **The Carrying of the Cross**
   Jesus carries the cross that will be used to crucify him.

5. **The Crucifixion**
   Jesus is nailed to the cross and dies.

The Glorious Mysteries

1. **The Resurrection**
   God the Father raises Jesus from the dead.

2. **The Ascension**
   Jesus returns to his Father in Heaven.

3. **The Coming of the Holy Spirit**
   The Holy Spirit comes to bring new life to the disciples.

4. **The Assumption of Mary**
   At the end of her life on earth, Mary is taken body and soul into Heaven.

5. **The Coronation of Mary**
   Mary is crowned as Queen of Heaven and Earth.

Stations of the Cross

The 14 Stations of the Cross represent events from Jesus' Passion and Death. At each station, we use our senses and imaginations to reflect prayerfully on the mystery of Jesus' suffering, Death, and Resurrection.

1

Jesus Is Condemned to Death.
Pontius Pilate condemns Jesus to death.

2

Jesus Takes Up His Cross.
Jesus willingly accepts and patiently bears his cross.

3

Jesus Falls the First Time.
Weakened by torments and loss of blood, Jesus falls beneath his cross.

4

Jesus Meets His Sorrowful Mother.
Jesus meets his mother, Mary, who is filled with grief.

5

Simon of Cyrene Helps Jesus Carry the Cross.
Soldiers force Simon of Cyrene to carry the cross.

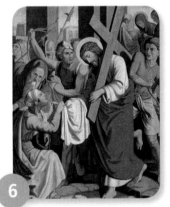

6

Veronica Wipes the Face of Jesus.
Veronica steps through the crowd to wipe the face of Jesus.

Continued Next Page

stations

Jesus Falls a Second Time.
Jesus falls beneath the weight of the cross a second time.

Jesus Meets the Women of Jerusalem.
Jesus tells the women not to weep for him but for themselves and their children.

Jesus Falls the Third Time.
Weakened almost to the point of death, Jesus falls a third time.

Jesus Is Stripped of His Garments.
The soldiers strip Jesus of his garments, treating him as a common criminal.

Jesus Is Nailed to the Cross.
Jesus' hands and feet are nailed to the cross.

Jesus Dies on the Cross.
After suffering greatly on the cross, Jesus bows his head and dies.

Jesus Is Taken Down from the Cross.
The lifeless body of Jesus is tenderly placed in the arms of Mary, his mother.

Jesus Is Laid in the Tomb.
Jesus' disciples place his body in the tomb.

The closing prayer—sometimes included as a 15th station—reflects on the Resurrection of Jesus.

glossary

A

adoration the act of giving reverence to God in body, mind, and soul. Recognizing and worshiping God in the Blessed Sacrament is often called adoration.

Anointing of the Sick one of the seven sacraments. In this sacrament a sick person has holy oil applied and receives the strength, peace, and courage to overcome the difficulties associated with illness. Through this sacrament Jesus brings the recipient spiritual healing and forgiveness of sins. If it is God's will, healing of the body is given as well.

apostolic the Mark of the Church that indicates that Jesus continues to lead the Church through the pope and the bishops. The pope and the bishops are the successors of the Apostles.

Assumption Mary's being taken, body and soul, into Heaven. Mary had a special relationship with her Son, Jesus, from the very beginning when she conceived him. Because of this relationship, she enjoys a special participation in Jesus' Resurrection and has been taken into Heaven where she now lives with him. We celebrate this event in the Feast of the Assumption on August 15.

B

Baptism the first of the seven sacraments. Baptism frees us from Original Sin and is necessary for Salvation. Baptism gives us new life in Jesus Christ through the Holy Spirit. The celebrant baptizes the person with water in the name of the Father, the Son, and the Holy Spirit.

baptismal promises the promises made by a person about to be baptized, or by the parents or godparents on behalf of an infant or a child unable to make promises on his or her own. The baptismal promises renounce Satan and commit the person to living a faithful Christian life.

Beatitudes the teachings of Jesus in the Sermon on the Mount in Matthew's Gospel. The Beatitudes are eight ways of living the Christian life. They are the fulfillment of the commandments given to Moses. These teachings present the way to true happiness.

Body of Christ In the Sacrament of the Eucharist, all the risen Lord Jesus Christ—body, blood, soul, and divinity—is present under the appearances of bread and wine. If a person receives only one element of the sacrament, that is, only the Body or only the Blood, that person still receives Jesus completely—body, blood, soul, and divinity.

C

canonized the state of a person who has been declared a saint by the Church. A canonized person has been found to have lived a holy and virtuous Christian life and has had two miracles attributed to his or her intercession.

Cardinal Virtues the four virtues that help a person live in relationship with God and with others: prudence, justice, fortitude, and temperance.

catholic one of the four Marks of the Church. The Church is catholic because Jesus is fully present in it, because it proclaims the fullness of faith, and because Jesus has given the Church to the whole world. The Church is universal.

centering prayer a popular form of contemplation that opens our heart to God's grace. Centering prayer uses a word or phrase to focus our mind and heart.

common good the sum total of the social conditions that allow people, individually and as a group, to reach their full potential. It requires peace, security, respecting everyone's rights, and meeting everyone's spiritual and worldly needs. People have a responsibility to contribute to the good of the entire society. It is one of the basic principles at the center of Catholic Social Teaching.

confession the act of telling our sins to a priest in the Sacrament of Penance and Reconciliation. The sacrament itself is sometimes referred to as confession.

Confirmation the sacrament that completes the grace we receive in Baptism. It seals, or confirms, this grace through the seven Gifts of the Holy Spirit that we receive as part of Confirmation. This sacrament also makes us better able to participate in the worship and apostolic life of the Church.

conscience the inner voice that helps each of us judge the morality of our own actions. It guides us to follow God's law by doing good and avoiding evil.

contemplation the act of prayerfully and continuously focusing on God. Many religious communities and spiritualities in the Church are devoted to contemplation.

contrition the sorrow we feel when we know that we have sinned, followed by the decision not to sin again. Contrition is the most important act of the penitent preparing to celebrate the Sacrament of Penance and Reconciliation.

Corporal Works of Mercy kind acts by which we help our neighbors with their everyday material needs. Corporal Works of Mercy include feeding the hungry, giving drink to the thirsty, finding a home for the homeless, clothing the naked, visiting the sick and those in prison, and burying the dead.

Creed a brief summary of what people believe. The word *creed* comes from the Latin *credo*, "I believe." The Nicene Creed and the Apostles' Creed are the most important summaries of Christian beliefs.

D

daily examen a prayerful meditation developed by Ignatius of Loyola that helps us see God at work in our daily lives. In the daily examen, we pray for light, give thanks, review the day, look at what we have done wrong, and make resolutions for the day to come.

E

Eucharist the sacrament in which we give thanks to God for giving us the Body and Blood of Christ. The risen Jesus Christ has Real Presence in the Eucharist. This means his body, blood, soul, and divinity are wholly and entirely present. We call the Real Presence of the risen Jesus Christ in the Eucharist transubstantiation.

F

faith a gift of God that helps us believe in him. We profess our faith in the Creed, celebrate it in the sacraments, live by it through our good conduct of loving God and our neighbor, and express it in prayer. It is a personal adherence of the whole person to God, who has revealed himself to us through words and actions throughout history.

Father the first Person of the Trinity as revealed to us by Jesus, his only begotten Son

Fathers of the Church the leaders of the Church in the first centuries after the time of the Apostles. The Fathers were important early thinkers and writers who continue to influence and inspire the Church.

free will the ability to choose to do good because we are made in the image of God. Our free will is what makes us truly human. Our exercise of free will to do good increases our freedom. Using free will to choose sin makes us slaves to sin.

G

godparents witnesses to Baptism who assume the responsibility for helping the baptized person along the road of Christian life

H

Holy Orders the sacrament through which the mission given by Jesus to his Apostles continues in the Church. The sacrament has three degrees: deacon, priest, and bishop. Through the laying on of hands in the Sacrament of Holy Orders, men receive a permanent sacramental mark that calls them to minister to the Church.

Holy Spirit the third Person of the Trinity, who is sent to us as our helper and, through Baptism and Confirmation, fills us with God's life. Together with the Father and the Son, the Holy Spirit brings the divine plan of Salvation to completion.

I

imaginative prayer a prayer that uses the Gospels or other Scripture readings to focus our thoughts on God and his will for our lives. In imaginative prayer, we can put ourselves in the situation from the passage to help make God present to us.

Immaculate Conception the Church teaching that Mary was free from Original Sin from the first moment of her conception. She was preserved through the merits of her Son, Jesus, the Savior of the human race. It was declared a dogma of the Catholic Church by Pope Pius IX in 1854 and is celebrated on December 8.

incense a sweet-smelling substance that is burned during the liturgy. Just as Jews burned incense to honor God in the Temple, the Church uses incense to honor him during worship. Incense ascends to God, reminding us of how our prayers rise up to Heaven.

intercede to pray on someone else's behalf, usually to fulfill some need. We can ask others to intercede for us, whether they are alive on earth or in Heaven with God.

intercession a prayer that asks for the fulfillment of another's needs. We can ask for the intercession of those in Heaven, such as Mary and the saints, or those still with us here on earth.

L

laity those who have been made members of Christ in Baptism and who participate in the priestly, prophetic, and kingly functions of Christ in his mission to the whole world. The laity is distinct from the clergy, whose members are set apart as ministers to serve the Church.

Law of Love, the the commandments of God that are a guide to loving God and other people. The Law of Love sets us free to live in the right way in accordance with the will of God.

liturgical year the celebration throughout the year of the mysteries of the Lord's birth, life, Death, Resurrection, and Ascension. The cycle of the liturgical year constitutes the basic rhythm of the Christian's life of prayer.

liturgy the public prayer of the Church that celebrates the wonderful things God has done for us in Jesus Christ, our high priest, and the way in which he continues the work of our Salvation. The original meaning of *liturgy* was "a public work or service done for the people."

M

Marks of the Church the main characteristics that distinguish the Church. The four Marks are the foundation of how we recognize the Catholic Church. The Church is *one, holy, catholic,* and *apostolic.*

Matrimony a solemn agreement between a woman and a man to be partners for life, for their own good and for bringing up children. Marriage is a sacrament when the agreement is properly made between baptized Christians.

meditation a form of prayer using silence and listening that seeks through imagination, emotion, and desire to understand how to adhere and respond to what God is asking. By concentrating on a word or an image, we move beyond thoughts, empty the mind of contents that get in the way of our experience of God, and rest in simple awareness of God.

mercy the gift to be able to respond to those in need with care and compassion. In always being ready to forgive our sins, God's mercy is a reality for us. The gift of mercy is a grace given to us by Jesus Christ.

mortal sin a serious decision to turn away from God by doing something that we know is wrong. For a sin to be mortal, it must be a very serious offense, the person must know how serious it is, and the person must freely choose to do it anyway.

O

Ordinary Time the periods of the Church calendar between the end of the Christmas season and Ash Wednesday and between the end of the Easter season and the beginning of Advent. Our growth as disciples in our commitment to Jesus is one focus of Ordinary Time.

Original Sin the consequence of the disobedience of the first human beings. They disobeyed God and chose to follow their own will rather than God's will. As a result, human beings lost the original blessing God had intended and became subject to sin and death. In Baptism we are restored to life with God through Jesus Christ, although we still experience the effects of Original Sin.

P

Paschal Mystery the work of Salvation accomplished by Jesus Christ through his Passion, Death, Resurrection, and Ascension. The Paschal Mystery is celebrated in the liturgy of the Church, and we experience its saving effects in the sacraments. In every liturgy of the Church, God the Father is blessed and adored as the source of all blessings we have received through his Son in order to make us his children through the Holy Spirit.

penance physical and spiritual acts that express our turning away from sin with a desire to change our lives and more closely live the way God wants us to live. We express our penance externally by praying, fasting, and helping those who are poor. Penance is also the name of the action that the priest asks us to take or the prayers that he asks us to pray after he absolves us in the Sacrament of Penance and Reconciliation.

Penance and Reconciliation the sacrament in which we celebrate God's forgiveness of sin and our reconciliation with God and the Church. Penance includes sorrow for the sins we have committed, confession of sins, absolution by the priest, and doing the penance that shows our willingness to amend our ways and atone for our sins.

penitent a person who is sorry for his or her sins. A person who receives the Sacrament of Penance and Reconciliation is known as a penitent.

Penitential Rite a formal ceremonial act that asks God's forgiveness for sin. Penitential Rites can be found in many liturgies, especially the Rite of Anointing of the Sick and in the Mass.

Pentecost the 50th day after Jesus was raised from the dead. On this day the Holy Spirit was sent from Heaven, and the Church was born. It is also a Jewish feast, called *Shavuot* in Hebrew, that celebrated the giving of the Ten Commandments on Mount Sinai 50 days after the Exodus.

People of God another name for the Church. In the same way that the people of Israel were God's people through the Covenant he made with them, the Church is a priestly, prophetic, and royal people through the new and eternal Covenant with Jesus Christ.

petition a request to God, asking him to fulfill a need. When we share in God's saving love, we understand that every need is one that we can ask God to help us with through petition.

pope the Bishop of Rome, successor of Saint Peter, and leader of the Roman Catholic Church. Because he has the authority to act in the name of Christ, the pope is called the Vicar of Christ. The pope and all the bishops together make up the living, teaching office of the Church, the Magisterium.

R

Real Presence the way in which the risen Jesus Christ is present in the Eucharist under the form of bread and wine. Jesus Christ's presence is called real because in the Eucharist his Body and Blood, soul and divinity, are wholly and entirely present. This is called transubstantiation.

Resurrection the bodily raising of Jesus Christ from the dead on the third day after his Death on the cross. The Resurrection is the crowning truth of our faith.

Revelation God's communication of himself to us through the words and deeds he has used throughout history to show us the mystery of his plan for our Salvation. This Revelation reaches its completion in his sending of his Son, Jesus Christ.

Rite of Christian Initiation of Adults (RCIA) the formal process by which adults become members of the Church. RCIA includes different types of spiritual formation that lead to Baptism, Confirmation, and receiving Holy Communion for the first time at the Easter Vigil.

S

sacramental an object, a prayer, or a blessing given by the Church to help us grow in our spiritual life

sacraments the seven official rites through which God's life enters our lives in the liturgy through the work of the Holy Spirit. Christ's work in the liturgy is sacramental because his mystery is made present there by the power of the Holy Spirit. Jesus gave us three sacraments that bring us into the Church: Baptism, Confirmation, and the Eucharist. He gave us two sacraments that bring us healing: Penance and Reconciliation and Anointing of the Sick. He also gave us two sacraments that help members serve the community: Matrimony and Holy Orders.

Sacraments of Initiation the sacraments that are the foundation of our Christian life. We are born anew in Baptism, strengthened by Confirmation, and receive in the Eucharist the food of eternal life. By means of these sacraments, we receive an increasing measure of the divine life and advance toward the perfection of charity.

Salvation the gift, which God alone can give, of forgiveness of sin and the restoration of friendship with him

Scripture the holy writings of Jews and Christians collected in the Old and New Testaments of the Bible

Sign of the Cross the gesture we make that signifies our belief in God the Father, the Son, and the Holy Spirit. It is a sign of blessing and a confession of faith, identifying us as followers of Jesus Christ.

sin a deliberate thought, word, deed, or failure to act that offends God and hurts our relationships with other people. Some sin is mortal and needs to be confessed in the Sacrament of Penance and Reconciliation. Other sin is venial, or less serious.

sins of commission a sin that is sinful because of something we do, such as stealing or lying

sins of omission a sin that is sinful because of something we fail to do when we have the responsibility to do so. We commit sins of omission when we stand by and do nothing when someone is being hurt, when we neglect our work, or when we fail to obey our parents or others in lawful authority.

solidarity the attitude of strength and unity that leads to the sharing of spiritual and material goods. Solidarity unites rich and poor, weak and strong, to foster a society in which all give what they can and receive what they need. The idea of solidarity is based on the common origin of all humanity.

Son the title revealed by Jesus that indicates his unique relationship to God the Father. The revelation of Jesus' divine sonship is the main dramatic development of the story of Jesus of Nazareth as it unfolds in the Gospels.

Spiritual Works of Mercy the kind acts through which we help our neighbors meet their needs that are more than material. The Spiritual Works of Mercy include counselling the doubtful, instructing the ignorant, admonishing sinners, comforting the afflicted, forgiving offenses, bearing wrongs patiently, and praying for the living and the dead.

spontaneous prayer the act of reflecting in our own words on our relationship with God or on his action in our lives. Spontaneous prayers can be of thanksgiving, petition, contrition, or meditation.

subsidiarity the principle that the best institutions for responding to a particular social task are those closest to it. It is the responsibility of the closest political or private institution to assist those in need. Only when issues cannot be resolved at the local level should they be resolved at a higher level.

T

Ten Commandments the ten rules given by God to Moses on Mount Sinai that sum up God's law and show us what is required to love God and our neighbor. By following the Ten Commandments, the Hebrews accepted their Covenant with God.

theologians experts in the study of God and his Revelation to the world

Theological Virtues the three virtues of faith, hope, and charity that are gifts from God and not acquired by human effort. The virtue of faith helps us believe in him, the virtue of hope helps us desire eternal life and the Kingdom of God, and the virtue of charity helps us love God and our neighbor as we should.

Tradition the beliefs and practices of the Church that are passed down from one generation to the next under the guidance of the Holy Spirit. What Christ entrusted to the Apostles was handed on to others both orally and in writing. Tradition and Scripture together make up the single deposit of faith, which remains present and active in the Church.

traditional prayers the prayers the Church has passed down through the centuries that enable people to pray in unison. The Psalms and the Rosary are examples of traditional prayers.

Trinity, Holy the mystery of the existence of God in the three Persons—the Father, the Son, and the Holy Spirit. Each Person is God, whole and entire. Each is distinct only in the relationship of each to the others. We follow Jesus, God the Son, because God the Father calls us and God the Holy Spirit moves us.

V

venial sin a choice we make that weakens our relationship with God or with other people. Venial sin wounds and lessens the divine life in us. If we make no effort to do better, venial sin can lead to more serious sin. Through our participation in the Eucharist, venial sin is forgiven when we are repentant, strengthening our relationship with God and with others.

vestments special symbolic garments used by bishops, priests, and deacons during the liturgy. The colors and designs of vestments remind us of the mysteries and truths of our faith.

viaticum the Eucharist that a sick or dying person receives. It is spiritual food for the last journey we make as Christians, the journey through death to eternal life.

virtues a firm attitude or way of acting that enables us to do good.

vocal prayer a prayer that uses words to talk to God. Vocal prayer is the most common and natural form of talking to God.

index

acknowledgments

Excerpts from the *New American Bible, revised edition* © 2010, 1991, 1986, 1970 Confraternity of Christian Doctrine, Washington, D.C. and are used by permission of the copyright owner. All rights reserved. No part of the *New American Bible* may be reproduced in any form without permission in writing from the copyright owner.

The English translation of the Act of Contrition from *Rite of Penance* © 1974, International Commission on English in the Liturgy Corporation (ICEL); the English translation of the *Memorare*, Queen of Heaven, and *Salve Regina* from *A Book of Prayers* © 1982, ICEL; the English translation of the Prayer Before Meals and Prayer After Meals from *Book of Blessings* © 1988, ICEL; the English translation of the Nicene Creed and Apostles' Creed from *The Roman Missal* © 2010, ICEL. All rights reserved.

The English translation of the *Magnificat* by the International Consultation on English Texts.

The Prayer to the Holy Spirit from the *United States Catholic Catechism for Adults,* © 2006, U.S. Conference of Catholic Bishops. Used with permission. All rights reserved.

Loyola Press has made every effort to locate the copyright holders for the cited works used in this publication and to make full acknowledgment for their use. In the case of any omissions, the publisher will be pleased to make suitable acknowledgments in future editions.

Art and Photography

When there is more than one picture on a page, positions are abbreviated as follows: **(t)** top, **(c)** center, **(b)** bottom, **(l)** left, **(r)** right, **(bg)** background, **(bd)** border.

Photos and illustrations not acknowledged are either owned by Loyola Press or from royalty-free sources including but not limited to Art Resource, Alamy, Bridgeman, Corbis/Veer, Getty Images, iStockphoto, Jupiterimages, Media Bakery, PunchStock, Shutterstock, Thinkstock, and Wikipedia Commons. Loyola Press has made every effort to locate the copyright holders for the cited works used in this publication and to make full acknowledgment for their use. In the case of any omissions, the publisher will be pleased to make suitable acknowledgments in future editions.

Frontmatter: iv–v Leungchopan/Dreamstime.com. **vi** Olga A/Shutterstock.com.

© iStockphoto.com: 1 Maica. **4** (c) dosrayitas. **4–5** (b) Maica. **6** (t) kirin_photo. **12–13** (b) Shanina. **19** johnwoodcock. **24** eyetoeyePIX. **26** (t) adl21. **26** (b) digitalhallway. **28** (ct) wynnter. **28** (cb) Jbryson. **30** (b) princessdlaf. **33** Nikada. **34** (t) contour99. **34** (b) laflor. **35** piccerella/Kathryn Seckman Kirsch. **35** piccerella/Kathryn Seckman Kirsch. **35** piccerella/Kathryn Seckman Kirsch. **36** (b) CEFutcher. **38** (b) digitalskillet. **48** juanestey. **50** (t) swilmor. **50** (b) DawnPoland. **54** (l, r) korinoxe. **54** (c) DraganSaponjic. **61** mikewesson. **62** (t) iPandastudio. **64** adl21. **67** (t) Moodboard_Images. **70** (t) jammydesign. **72** Pixel_Pig. **74** (t) RonBailey **74** (b) Juanmonino. **75** bubaone. **78** (cr) qingwa. **81** (t) jrroman. **86** (f) princessdlaf. **86** (g) sebastianiov. **88** princessdlaf. **93** LordRunar.

Thinkstock: 6 (b) iStockphoto. **10** iStockphoto. **12** (t) iStockphoto. **20** (b) Hemera. **28** (b) Comstock. **37** (b) iStockphoto. **41** Noel Hendrickson/Digital Vision. **42** (t) Martin Poole/Digital Vision. **43** (b) iadamson. **58** Hemera. **67** (b) iStockphoto.

Chapter 1: 2 Mel Curtis/Photodisc. **3** Fancy Photography/ Veer. **4** (t) Warling Studios. **7** "Abraham, Stained Glass, Mt. Olivet Lutheran Church, Minneapolis MN. The Crosiers/ Gene Plaisted, OSC." **8** Granger Wootz/Media Bakery.

Chapter 2: 11 The Crosiers/Gene Plaisted, OSC. **13** (t) Asia Images Group Pte Ltd/Alamy. **14** (t) Ocean Photography/ Veer. **14** (b) Warling Studios. **15** Saint Patrick, Laura James, 2011, (acrylic on wood). Private Collection/The Bridgeman Art Library International. **16** Alloy Photography/Veer.

Chapter 3: 17 Fancy Photography/Veer. **18** Jupiterimages. **20** (t) Pjcross/Veer. **21** (t) vadim kozlovsky/Shutterstock. com. **21** (b) Bill Perry/Shutterstock.com. **22** (t) testing/ Shutterstock.com. **22** (b) Warling Studios. **23** St. Paul, mosaic, Notre Dame Church, Louviers, France. The Crosiers/ Gene Plaisted, OSC.

Chapter 4: 25 LWA/Dann Tardif/Media Bakery. **27** Pascal Deloche/Godong/Corbis. **28** (t) W.P. Wittman Limited. **29** Loyola Press Photography. **30** (t) Private Collection/The Bridgeman Art Library International. **31** Pierre Toussaint, 1825 (w/c on ivory), Meucci, Anthony (fl.1825)/© Collection of the New-York Historical Society, USA/The Bridgeman Art Library International. **32** Ocean Photography/Veer.

Chapter 5: 36 (t) W.P. Wittman Limited. **37** (t) W.P. Wittman Limited. **38** (t) Warling Studios. **39** Guiseppe Sarto, Pope Pius X (1835–1914). Herbert Barraud/Stringer/ Hulton Archive/Getty Images. **40** Ocean Photography/Veer.

Chapter 6: 42 (b) Rubberball/Alan Bailey/Getty Images. **43** (br) Aaron Amat/Shutterstock.com. **44** (t) Caro/ Alamy. **44** (b) Image Source/Getty Images. **45** (t) Phil Martin Photography. **45** (b) blackpixel/Shutterstock.com. **46** (t) W.P. Wittman Limited. **46** (b) Rafael Lopez. **47** Mary MacKillop,1882, photo released by The Trustess of the Sisters of St. Joseph. AFP/Stringer/Getty Images.

Chapter 7: 52 Warling Studios. **53** (t) Kathryn Seckman Kirsch. **53** (b) P Deliss/Corbis. **55** St. Augustine in his Cell, Sandro Botticelli, c.1480, Ognissanti, Florence, Italy. Giraudon/The Bridgeman Art Library International. **56** Corbis Photography/Veer.

Chapter 8: 57 okea/Veer. **59** Private Collection/ The Bridgeman Art Library International. **60** Alloy Photography/Veer. **62** (b) Warling Studios. **63** Ignatius of Loyola, 1500s. Alfgar/Shutterstock.com.

Chapter 9: 65 Creatista/Veer. **66** (t) Perov Stanislav/ Shutterstock.com. **66** (b) Warling Studios. **68** Warling Studios. **69** W.P. Wittman Limited. **70** (b) Warling Studios. **71** St. Stephen's Episcopal Church, Orinda CA. The Crosiers/ Gene Plaisted, OSC.

Chapter 10: 76 (t) Copyright © 2009 by The Chicago, Detroit, and Wisconsin Provinces of the Society of Jesus. **76** (b) IFK photo/Alamy. **77** Ian Shipley PRD/ Alamy. **78** (t) Warling Studios. **78** (cl) Royalty-free image. **78** (b) W.P. Wittman Limited. **79** Saint Thérèse of Lisieux, at 15 years,1818. © Office Central de Lisieux. **80** Alloy Photography/Veer.

Catholic Beliefs and Practices: 81 (b) The Crosiers/Gene Plaisted, OSC. **82** Johnny van Haeften Gallery, London, UK/ The Bridgeman Art Library International. **83** (t) Zacarias Pereira da Mata/Shutterstock.com. **83** (b) Stockbyte/ Getty Images. **84** Hermitage, St. Petersburg, Russia/The Bridgeman Art Library International. **85** (t) moodboard Photography/Veer. **85** (b) Birgid Allig/Media Bakery. **86** Clockwise from upper left, (a) platayregalo.com. **86** (b) Greg Kuepfer. **86** (c) Royalty-free image. **86** (d) Permission of CM Almy. **86** (e) Loyola Press Photography. **87** Warling Studios. **89** (t) Private Collection/The Bridgeman Art Library International. **89** (b) Warling Studios. **90** (t) Media Bakery. **90** (b) Royalty-free image. **91** OJO Images Photography/ Veer. **94** (t) Roberto Cerruti/Shutterstock.com. **94** (b) Warling Studios. **95** Greg Kuepfer. **96** © 2012 Con Tanasiuk/ Design Pics. **97** (tl) Zvonimir Atletic/Shutterstock.com. **97** (tc) Zvonimir Atletic/Shutterstock.com. **97** (tr) Zvonimir Atletic/Shutterstock.com. **97** (bl) Zvonimir Atletic/ Shutterstock.com. **97** (bc) Zvonimir Atletic/Shutterstock. com. **97** (br) Zvonimir Atletic/Shutterstock.com. **98** (tl) Zvonimir Atletic/Shutterstock.com. **98** (tc) Zvonimir Atletic/ Shutterstock.com. **98** (tr) Zvonimir Atletic/Shutterstock. com. **98** (cl) Zvonimir Atletic/Shutterstock.com. **98** (c) Zvonimir Atletic/Shutterstock.com. **98** (cr) Zvonimir Atletic/ Shutterstock.com. **98** (bl) Zvonimir Atletic/Shutterstock.com. **98** (br) Zvonimir Atletic/Shutterstock.com.